The

Kuzari Book

Rebbi
Yehuda Halevi

Translated To Hebrew By

Rebbi
Yehuda Ben Tibbon

Translated to English by Itzhak H. Aboudi

There is no known book without mistakes. Therefore, I ask in every language of application if anyone has any questions, comments, clarifications, corrections, please send to: **simchatchaim@yahoo.com**

All material used in this section may not be used for commercial purposes, but only for study and teaching.

To get this book or books and information Email me at:

simchatchaim@yahoo.com

Copyright©All Rights Reserved to

www.simchatchaim.com

YB"S©All rights reserved to the Editor

First Edition 2023

Content of the book

3. The Kuzari Book

7. First Essay

67. Second Essay

133. Third Essay

211. Fourth Essay

273. Fifth Essay

The cover of the book of the **Kuzari**
Printed in Warsaw in the year 1827

Kuzari   הַכּוּזָרִי

The Kuzari Book

Rebbi Yehuda Halevi (also Yehuda Halevi or ha-Levi; Hebrew: יהודה הלוי and Yehuda ben Shmuel Halevi יהודה בן שמואל הלוי; Arabic: يهوذا اللاوي Yahuda al-Lawi; c. 1075 – 1141) was a Spanish Jewish physician, poet and philosopher. He was born in Spain, either in Toledo or Tudela, in 1075 or 1086, and died shortly after arriving in the Holy Land in 1141, at that point the Crusader Kingdom of Yerusalem.

Rebbi Yehuda Halevi is considered one of the greatest Hebrew poets, celebrated both for his religious and secular poems, many of which appear in present-day liturgy. His greatest philosophical work was the - **The Kuzari Book**

It is the philosophical work of Rebbi Yehuda Halevi [Riha"l], written in the year 1139 in Jewish Arabic. The Jewish sage Rebbi Yehuda Ben Tibbon translated this book from Arabic to Hebrew. The first Hebrew of the book was called "**The Kuzari Book**" and thus acquired its famous name. The book is written in the form of a conversation between the king of the Khazars and a Jewish sage about the foundations of Judaism. The story of the voluntary conversion of the Khazars several

Kuzari   הכוזרי

generations earlier serves the author as a background and basis for the character of a Khazar king. The Kuzari book is considered one of the pillars of Jewish philosophy in particular, and of Jewish thought in general.

The book, which consists of five parts, is written in five essays. It describes and protects the tenets of the Jewish faith, at a time when Judaism is between the Christian hammer and the Muslim anvil, and in an attack of both parts of philosophy and on the part of the Karaites [Group of Jews who left Judaism who refused to follow the Sages]. The book makes external-frame use of the Platonic methodology of dialogue, with a slightly different interpretation of the concept of the dialogue, and from an internal-perceptual point of view Rebbi Yehuda Halevi who often uses Aristotelian conceptions, despite his principled opposition to them, to illustrate the ideas he presents.

By way of dialogues between the king of the Khazars who is looking for a new religion, and the Jewish sage who describes Judaism to him, Rebbi Yehuda Halevi shows a whole foundation of the Jewish faith that is not based on cold philosophical logic, but on historical prophetic revelation, which does not contradict rational thinking here. Through the questions and investigations of King Kuzor, Rebbi Yehuda Halevi confronts different religions,

Kuzari   הכוזרי

beliefs, and philosophical opinions, and presents the position of Judaism on these issues, according to his interpretation. In contrast to theoretical philosophical books, this book is vibrant and alive and challenges the reader to continue reading it due to its form, style, and content. Rebbi Yehuda Halevi's deep knowledge of the virtues of Judaism, his broad philosophical education, as well as his scientific understanding and profession [physician] are evident in the book.

The book opens with the dream of a Kuzor king, in which he sees an angel informing him: "Your intention is desirable, but the deed is not desirable." This dream comes back to him several times. Since the king maintains the Khazar religion in its entirety, he understands that he will have to look for the desired deed elsewhere. He first met with non -Jewish philosopher. King Kuzor agrees with the philosopher's logical and consistent words but they contradict the dream words, as the king seeks the desired deed. While the philosopher claims that God has no will and does not oversee human beings of the other religions, the king precedes the encounter with the Christian. The Christian answers do not settle on his heart, for they do not depend on logic and wisdom, and they are worthy of one who has been educated by them since childhood or foresaw in his eyes the same signs. In his

Kuzari

encounter with the Muslim sage, he does not accept the possibility of the existence of a universal religion written in a national language. Having no choice, and seeing that the major religions nurture from it. He examines Judaism - the "despicable religion" - and meets with a Jewish Rebbi. He finds meaning in his words and often inquires and asks him questions. Following this, the king and all his people are converted. The king continues to discuss with the Rebbi even after his conversion.

The Kuzair argument is a famous Jewish example of an attempt to base the righteousness of religion through tradition on an experience of revelation or a miracle experience that did occur.

First Essay

The author Yehuda ben Shaul said, I Waw asked to state what arguments and replies I could bring to bear against the attacks of philosophers and followers of other religions, and also against Jewish sectarians who attacked the rest of Israel. This reminded me of something I had once heard concerning the arguments of a Rebbi who sojourned with the King of the Khazars. The latter, as we know from historical records, became a convert to Judaism about four hundred years ago. To him came a dream, and it appeared as if an angel addressed him, saying: 'Thy way of thinking is indeed pleasing to the Creator, but not thy way of acting.' Yet he was so zealous in the performance of the Khazar religion, that he devoted himself with a perfect heart to the service of the temple and sacrifices. Notwithstanding this devotion, the angel came again at night and repeated: 'Thy way of thinking is pleasing to God, but not thy way of acting.' This caused him to ponder over the different beliefs and religions, and finally become a convert to Judaism together with many other Khazars. As I found among the arguments of the Rebbi, many which appealed to me, and were in harmony with my own opinions, I resolved to write them down exactly as they had been spoken. When the King of Khazar as is related dreamt that his way of thinking was agreeable to God, but not his way of acting, and was commanded in the same dream to seek the God-pleasing work, he inquired of a philosopher concerning his religious persuasion.

1. The philosopher replied: There is no favor or dislike in the nature of God, because He is above desire and intention. A desire intimates a want in the person who feels it, and not till it is satisfied does he become so to speak complete. If it remains unfulfilled, he lacks completion. In a similar way He is, in the opinion of philosophers, above the knowledge of individuals, because the latter change with the times, whilst there is no change in God's knowledge. He, therefore, does not know thee, much less thy thoughts and actions, nor does He listen to thy prayers, or see thy movements. If philosophers say that He created thee, they only use a metaphor, because He is the Cause of causes in the creation of all creatures, but not because this was His intention from the beginning. He never created man. For the world is without beginning, and there never arose a man otherwise than through one who came into existence before him, in whom were united forms, gifts, and characteristics inherited from father, mother, and other relations, besides the influences of climate, countries, foods and water, spheres, stars and constellations. Everything is reduced to a Prime Cause; not to a Will proceeding from this, but an Emanation from which emanated a second, a third, and fourth cause. The Cause and the caused are, as you see, intimately connected with one another, their coherence being as eternal as the Prime Cause and having no beginning. Every individual on earth has his completing causes; consequently, an individual with perfect causes becomes perfect, and another with imperfect causes remains imperfect, as the negro who is able to receive nothing more than the human shape and speech in its least developed form. The philosopher, however, who is equipped with the highest capacity, receives through it the advantages of disposition, intelligence and active power, so that he wants nothing to make him perfect. Now these perfections exist but in abstract, and require instruction and training to become practical, and in order that this capacity, with all its completeness or deficiencies and endless grades, may become visible. In the perfect person a light of divine nature, called Active Intellect, is with him, and its Passive Intellect is so closely connected therewith that both are but one. The person of such perfection thus observes that he is The Active Intellect himself, and that there is no difference between them. His organs-I mean the limbs of such a person-only serve for the most perfect purposes, in the most appropriate time, and in the best condition, as if they were the organs of the Active Intellect, but not of the material and passive Intellect, which used them at an earlier period, sometimes well, but more often improperly. The Active Intellect, however, is always successful. This degree is the last and most longed-for goal for the perfect man whose soul, after having been purified, has grasped the inward truths of all branches of science, has thus become equal to an angel, and has found a place on the nethermost step of seraphic beings. This is the degree of the Active Intellect, viz. that angel whose degree is below the angel who is connected with the sphere of the moon. There are spiritual forces, detached from matter, but eternal like the Prime Cause and never threatened by decay. Thus, the soul of the perfect man and that Intellect become One, without concern for the decay of his body or his organs, because he becomes united to the other. His soul is cheerful while he is alive, because it enjoys the company of Hermes, Asclepios, Socrates, Plato and Aristotle; nay, he and they, as well as every one who shares their degree, and the Active Intellect, are one thing. This is what is called allusively and approximately Pleasure of God. Endeavor to reach it, and the true knowledge of things, in order that thy intellect may become active, but not passive. Keep just ways as regards character and actions, because this will help thee to effect truth, to gain instruction, and to become similar to this Active Intellect. The consequence of this will be contentment, humility, meekness, and every other praiseworthy inclination, accompanied by the veneration of the Prime Cause, not in order to receive favor from it, or to divert its wrath, but solely to become like the Active Intellect in finding the truth, in describing everything in a fitting manner, and in rightly recognizing its basis. These are the characteristics of the Active Intellect. If thou hast reached such disposition of belief, be not concerned about the forms of thy humility or religion or worship, or the word or language or actions you employ. You may even choose a religion in the way of humility, worship, and benediction, for the management of thy temperament, thy house and the people of thy country, if they agree to it. Or fashion thy religion according to the laws of reason set up by philosophers, and strive after purity of soul. In fine, seek purity of heart in which way thou art able, provided thou hast acquired the sum total of knowledge in its real essence; then thou wilt reach thy goal, viz. the union with this Spiritual, or rather Active Intellect. Maybe he will communicate with thee or teach thee the knowledge of what is hidden through true dreams and positive visions.

2. Said to him the Khazari: Your words are

convincing, yet they do not correspond to what I wish to find. I know already that my soul is pure and that my actions are calculated to gain the favor of God. To all this I received the answer that this way of action does not find favor, though the intention does. There must no doubt be a way of acting, pleasing by its very nature, but not through the medium of intentions. If this be not so, why, then, do Christian and Muslim, who divide the inhabited world between them, fight with one another, each of them serving his God with pure intention, living either as monks or hermits, fasting and praying? For all that they vie with each other in committing murders, believing that this is a most pious work and brings them nearer to God. They fight in the belief that paradise and eternal bliss will be their reward. It is, however, impossible to agree with both.

3. The Philosopher replied: The philosophers' creed knows no manslaughter, as they only cultivate the intellect.

4. Al Khazari: What could be more erroneous, in the opinion of the philosophers, than the belief that the world was created in six days, or that the Prime Cause spoke with mortals, not to mention the philosophic doctrine, which declares the former to be above knowing details. In addition to this one might expect the gift of prophecy quite common among philosophers, considering their deeds, their knowledge, their researches after truth, their exertions, and their close connection with all things spiritual, also that wonders, miracles, and extraordinary things would be reported of them. Yet we find that true visions are granted to persons who do not devote themselves to study or to the purification of their souls, whereas the opposite is the case with those who strive after these things. This proves that the divine influence as well as the souls have a secret which is not identical with what you say, O Philosopher.

4. After this the Khazari said to himself: I will ask the Christians and Muslims, since one of these persuasions is, no doubt, the God-pleasing one. As regards the Jews, I am satisfied that they are of low station, few in number, and generally despised.

He then invited a Christian scholastic, and put questions to him concerning the theory and practice of his faith.

The Scholastic replied: I believe that all things are created, whilst the Creator is eternal; that He created the whole world in six days; that all mankind sprang from Adam, and after him from Noah, to whom they trace themselves back; that God takes care of the created beings, and keeps in touch with man; that He shows wrath, pleasure, and compassion; that He speaks, appears, and reveals Himself to His prophets and favored ones; that He dwells among those who please him In short I believe in all that is written in the Torah and the records of the Children of Israel, which are undisputed, because they are generally known as lasting, and have been revealed before a vast multitude. Subsequently the divine essence became embodied in an embryo in the womb of a virgin taken from the noblest ranks of Israelite women. She bore Him with the semblance of a human being, but covering a divinity, seemingly a prophet, but in reality, a God sent forth. He is the MASHIACH, whom we call the Son of God, and He is the Father, and the Son and the Holy Spirit. We condense His nature into one thing, although the Trinity appears on our tongues. We believe in Him and in His abode among the Children of Israel, granted to them as a distinction, because the divine influence never ceased to be attached to them, until the masses rebelled against this MASHIACH, and they crucified Him. Then divine wrath burdened them everlastingly, while the favor was confined to a few who followed the MASHIACH, and to those nations which followed these few. We belong to their number. Although we are not of Israelite descent, we are well deserving of being called Children of Israel, because we follow the

MASHIACH and His twelve Israelite companions who took the place of the tribes. Many Israelites followed these twelve apostles, and became the leaven, as it were, for the Christians. We are worthy of the degree of the Children of Israel. To us was also granted victory, and expansion over the countries. All nations are invited to this religion, and charged to practice it, to adore the MASHIACH and the cross on which He was put, and the like. Our laws and regulations are derived from the Apostle Simon, and from ordinations taken from the Torah, which we study. Its truth is indisputable, as is also the fact that it came from God. It is also stated in the New Testament: I came not to destroy one of the laws of Moses, but I came to confirm and enlarge it.

5. Then said the Khazari: I see here no logical conclusion; nay, logic rejects most of what thou sayest. If both appearance and experience are so palpable that they take hold of the whole heart, compelling belief in a thing of which one is not convinced they render the matter more feasible by a semblance of logic. This is how natural philosophers deal with strange phenomena which come upon them unawares, and which they would not believe if they only heard of them without seeing them. When they have examined them, they discuss them, and ascribe them to the influence of stars or spirits without disproving ocular evidence. As for me, I cannot accept these things, because they come upon me suddenly, not having grown up in them. My duty is to investigate further.

He then invited one of the Doctors of Islam, and questioned him regarding his doctrine and observance.

The Doctor said: We acknowledge the unity and eternity of God, and that all men are derived from Adam Noah. We absolutely reject embodiment, and if any element of this appears in the Writ, we explain it as a metaphor and allegory. At the same time, we maintain that our Book is the Speech of God, being a miracle which we are bound to accept for its own sake, since no one is able to bring anything similar to it, or to one of its verses. Our prophet is the Seal of the prophets, who abrogated every previous law, and invited all nations to embrace Islam. The reward of the pious consists in the return of his spirit to his body in paradise and bliss, where he never ceases to enjoy eating, drinking, woman's love, and anything he may desire. The requital of the disobedient consists in being condemned to the fire of hell, and his punishment knows no end.

6. Said to him the Khazari: If any one is to be guided in matters divine, and to be convinced that God speaks to man, whilst he considers it improbable, he must be convinced of it by means of generally known facts, which allow no refutation, and particularly imbue him with the belief that God has spoken to man. Although your book may be a miracle, as long as it is written in Arabic, a non-Arab, as I am, cannot perceive its miraculous character; and even if it were read to me, I could not distinguish between it and any other book written in the Arabic language.

7. The Doctor replied: Yet miracles were performed by him, but they were not used as evidence for the acceptance of his law.

8. Al Khazari: Exactly so; but the human mind cannot believe that God has intercourse with man, except by a miracle which changes the nature of things. He then recognizes that to do so He alone is capable who created them from nought. It must also have taken place in the presence of great multitudes, who saw it distinctly, and did not learn it from reports and traditions. Even then they must examine the matter carefully and repeatedly, so that no suspicion of imagination or magic can enter their minds. Then it is possible that the mind may grasp this extraordinary matter, viz. that the Creator of this world and the next, of the heavens and lights, should hold intercourse with this contemptible piece of clay, I mean man, speak to him, and fulfil his wishes and desires.

9. The Doctor: Is not our Book full of the stories of Moshe and the Children of Israel? No one can deny what He did to Pharaoh, how He divided the sea, saved those who enjoyed His favour, but drowned those who had aroused His wrath. Then came the manna and the quails during forty years, His speaking to Moshe on the mount, making the sun stand still for Yehoshua, and assisting him against the mighty. Add to this what happened previously, viz. the Flood, the destruction of the people of Lot; is this not so well known that no suspicion of deceit and imagination is possible.

11. The Rebbi replied: I believe in the God of Abraham, Isaac and Israel, who led the children of Israel out of Egypt with signs and miracles; who fed them in the desert and gave them the land, after having made them traverse the sea and the Jordan in a miraculous way; who sent Moshe with His law, and subsequently thousands of prophets, who confirmed His law by promises to the observant, and threats to the disobedient. Our belief is comprised in the Torah-a very large domain.

11. The Rebbi replied: I believe in the God of Abraham, Itzhak and Israel, who led the children of Israel out of Egypt with signs and miracles; who fed them in the desert and gave them the land, after having made them traverse the sea and the Jordan in a miraculous way; who sent Moshe with His law, and subsequently thousands of prophets, who confirmed His law by promises to the observant, and threats to the disobedient. Our belief is comprised in the Torah-a very large domain.

12. Al Khazari: I had not intended to ask any Jew, because I am aware of their reduced condition and narrow-minded views, as their misery left them nothing commendable. Now shouldst thou, O Jew, not have said that thou believest in the Creator of the world, its Governor and Guide, and in Him who created and keeps thee, and such attributes which serve as evidence for every believer, and for the sake of which He pursues justice in order to resemble the Creator in His wisdom and justice.

13. The Rebbi: That which thou dost express is religion based on speculation and system, the research of thought, but open to many doubts. Now ask the philosophers, and thou wilt find that they do not agree on one action or one principle, since some doctrines can be established by arguments, which are only partially satisfactory, and still much less capable of being proved.

14. Al Khazari: That which thou sayest now, O Jew, seems to be more to the point than the beginning, and I should like to hear more.

15. The Rebbi: Surely the beginning of my speech was just the proof, and so evident that it requires no other argument.

16. Al Khazari: How so.

17. The Rebbi: Allow me to make a few preliminary remarks, for I see thee disregarding and depreciating my words.

18. Al Khazari: Let me hear thy remarks.

19. The Rebbi: If thou wert told that the King of India was an excellent man, commanding admiration, and deserving his high reputation, one whose actions were reflected in the justice which rules his country and the virtuous ways of his subjects, would this bind thee to revere him?

20. Al Khazari: How could this bind me, whilst I am not sure if the justice of the Indian people is natural, and not dependent on their king, or due to the king or both.

21. The Rebbi: But if his messenger came to thee bringing presents which thou knowest to be only procurable in India, and in the royal palace, accompanied by a letter in which it is distinctly stated from whom it comes, and to which are added drugs to cure thy diseases, to preserve thy health, poisons for thy enemies, and other means to fight and kill them without battle, would this make thee beholden to him?

22. Al Khazari: Certainly. For this would remove my former doubt that the Indians have a king. I should also acknowledge that a proof of his power and dominion has reached me.

23. The Rebbi: How wouldst thou, then, if asked, describe him.

24. Al Khazari: In terms about which I am quite clear, and to these I could add others which were at first rather doubtful, but are no longer so.

25. The Rebbi: In this way I answered thy first question. In the same strain spoke Moshe to Pharaoh, when he told him: 'The God of the Hebrews sent me to thee,' viz. the God of Abraham, Itzhak and Yaakov. For Abraham was well known to the nations, who also knew that the divine spirit was in contact with the patriarchs, cared for them, and performed miracles for them. He did not say: 'The God of heaven and earth,' nor 'my Creator and thine sent me.' In the same way God commenced His speech to the assembled people of Israel: 'I am the God whom you worship, who has led you out of the land of Egypt,' but He did not say: 'I am the Creator of the world and your Creator.' Now in the same style I spoke to thee, a Prince of the Khazars, when thou didst ask me about my creed. I answered thee as was fitting, and is fitting for the whole of Israel who knew these things, first from personal experience, and afterwards through uninterrupted tradition, which is equal to the former.

26. Al Khazari: If this be so, then your belief is confined to yourselves.

27. The Rebbi: Yes; but any Gentile who joins us unconditionally shares our good fortune, without, however, being quite equal to us. If the Law were binding on us only because God created us, the white and the black man would be equal, since He created them all. But the Law was given to us because He led us out of Egypt, and remained attached to us, because we are the pick of mankind.

28. Al Khazari: Jew, I see thee quite altered, and thy words are poor after having been so pleasant.

29. The Rebbi: Poor or pleasant, give me thy attention, and let me express myself more fully.

30. Al Khazari: Say what thou wilt.

31. The Rebbi: The laws of nature comprise nurture, growth, and propagation, with their powers and all conditions attached thereto. This is particularly the case with plants and animals, to the exclusion of earth, stones, metals, and elements.

32. Al Khazari: This is a maxim which requires explanation, though it be true.

33. The Rebbi: As regards the soul, it is given to all animated beings. The result is movement, will power, external as well as internal senses and such like.

34. Al Khazari: This, too, cannot be contradicted.

35. The Rebbi: Intellect is man's birthright above all living beings. This leads to the development of his faculties, his home, his country, from which arise administrative and regulative laws.

36. Al Khazari: This is also true.

37. The Rebbi: Which is the next highest degree.

38. Al Khazari: The degree of great sages.

39. The Rebbi: I only mean that degree which

separates those who occupy it from the physical point of view, as the plant is separated from inorganic things, or man from animals. The differences as to quantity, however, are endless, as they are only accidental, and do not really form a degree.

40. Al Khazari: If this be so, then there is no degree above man among tangible things.

41. The Rebbi: If we find a man who walks into the fire without hurt, or abstains from food for some time without starving, on whose face a light shine which the eye cannot bear, who is never ill, nor ages, until having reached his life's natural end, who dies spontaneously just as a man retires to his couch to sleep on an appointed day and hour, equipped with the knowledge of what is hidden as to past and future: is such a degree not visibly distinguished from the ordinary human degree.

42. Al Khazari: This is, indeed, the divine and seraphic degree, if it exists at all. It belongs to the province of the divine influence, but not to that of the intellectual, human, or natural world.

43. The Rebbi: These are some of the characteristics of the undoubted prophets through whom God made Himself manifest, and who also made known that there is a God who guides them as He wishes, according to their obedience or disobedience. He revealed to those prophets that which was hidden, and taught them how the world was created, how the generations prior to the Flood followed each other, and how they reckoned their descent from Adam. He described the Flood and the origin of the **Seventy Nations** from Shem, Ham and Japheth, the sons of Noah; how the languages were split up, and where men sought their habitations; how arts arose, how they built cities, and the chronology from Adam up to this day.

44. Al Khazari: It is strange that you should possess authentic chronology of the creation of the world.

45. The Rebbi: Surely, we reckon according to it, and there is no difference between the Jews of Khazar and Ethiopia in this respect.

46. Al Khazari: What date do you consider it at present?

47. The Rebbi: Four thousand and nine hundred years. The details can be demonstrated from the lives of Adam, Seth and Enosh to Noah; then Shem and Eber to Abraham; then Itzhak and Yaakov to Moshe. All of them represented the essence and purity of Adam on account of their intimacy with God. Each of them had children only to be compared to them outwardly, but not really like them, and, therefore, without direct union with the divine influence. The chronology was established through the medium of those sainted persons who were only single individuals, and not a crowd, until Yaakov begat the Twelve Tribes, who were all under this divine influence. Thus, the divine element reached a multitude of persons who carried the records further. The chronology of those who lived before these has been handed down to us by Moshe.

48. Al Khazari: An arrangement of this kind removes any suspicion of untruth or common plot. Not ten people could discuss such a thing without disagreeing, and disclosing their secret understanding; nor could they refute any one who tried to establish the truth of a matter like this. How is it possible where such a mass of people is concerned? Finally, the period involved is not large enough to admit untruth and fiction.

49. The Rebbi: That is so. Abraham himself lived during the period of the separation of languages. He and his relatives retained the language of his grandfather Eber, which for that reason is called Hebrew. Four hundred years after him appeared Moshe at a time when the world was rich in information concerning the heavens and earth. He approached Pharaoh and the Doctors of Egypt, as well as those of the Israelites. Whilst agreeing with him they questioned him, and completely refused to believe that God spoke with man, until he caused them to hear the Ten Words. In the same way the people were on his side, not from ignorance, but on account of the knowledge they possessed. They feared magic and astrological arts, and similar snares, things which, like deceit, do not bear close examination, whereas the divine might is like pure gold, ever increasing in brilliancy. How could one imagine that an attempt had been made to show that a language spoken five hundred years previously was none but Eber's own language split up in Babel during the days of Peleg; also, to trace the origin of this or that nation back to Shem or Ham, and the same with their countries? Is it likely that any one could to-day invent false statements concerning the origin, history, and languages of well-known nations, the latter being less than five hundred years old?

50. Al Khazari: This is not possible. How could it be, since we possess books in the handwriting of their authors written five hundred years ago? No false interpolation could enter the contents of a book which is not above five hundred years of age, such as genealogical tables, linguistic and other works.

51. The Rebbi: Now why should Moshe speeches remain uncontradicted? Did not his own people raise objections, not to speak of others.

52. Al Khazari: These things are handed down well founded and firmly established.

53. The Rebbi: Dost thou think that the languages are eternal and without beginning.

54. Al Khazari: No; they undoubtedly had a beginning, which originated in a conventional manner. Evidence of this is found in their composition of nouns, verbs, and particles. They originated from sounds derived from the organs of speech.

55. The Rebbi: Didst thou ever see any one who contrived a language, or didst thou hear of him.

56. Al Khazari: Neither the one nor the other. There is no doubt that it appeared at some time, but prior to this there was no language concerning which one nation, to the exclusion of another, could come to any agreement.

57. The Rebbi: Didst thou ever hear of a nation which possessed different traditions with regard to the generally acknowledged week which begins with the Sunday and ends with the Sabbath? How is it possible that the people of China could agree with those of the western islands without common beginning, agreement and convention.

58. Al Khazari: Such a thing would only have been possible if they had all come to an agreement. This, however, is improbable, unless all men are the descendants of Adam, of Noah, or of some other ancestor from whom they received the hebdomadal calculation.

59. The Rebbi: That is what I meant. East and West agree on the decimal system. What instinct. induced them to keep to the number ten, unless it was a tradition handed down by the first one who did so.

60. Al Khazari: Does it not weaken thy belief if thou art told that the Indians have antiquities and buildings which they consider to be millions of years old.

61. The Rebbi: It would, indeed, weaken my belief had they a fixed form of religion, or a book concerning which a multitude of people held the same opinion, and in which no historical discrepancy could be found. Such a book, however, does not exist. Apart from this, they are a dissolute, unreliable people, and arouse the indignation of the followers of religions through their talk, whilst they anger them with their idols, talismans, and witchcraft. To such things they pin their faith, and deride those who boast of the possession of a divine book. Yet they only possess a few books, and these were written to mislead the weak-minded. To this class belong astrological writings, in which they speak of ten thousand of years, as the book on the Nabataean Agriculture, in which are mentioned the names of Janbushar, Sagrit and Roanai. It is believed that they lived before Adam, who was the disciple of Janbushar, and such like.

62. Al Khazari: If I had supported my arguments by reference to a negro people, a people not united upon a common law, thy answer would have been correct. Now what is thy opinion of the philosophers who, as the result of their careful researches, agree that the world is without beginning, and here it does not concern tens of thousands, and not millions, but unlimited numbers of years.

63. The Rebbi: There is an excuse for the Philosophers. Being Grecians, science and religion did not come to them as inheritances. They belong to the descendants of Japheth, who inhabited the north, whilst that knowledge coming from Adam, and supported by the divine influence, is only to be found among the progeny of Shem, who represented the successors of Noah and constituted, as it were, his essence. This knowledge has always been connected with this essence, and will always remain so. The Greeks only received it when they became powerful, from Persia. The Persians had it from the Chaldaeans. It was only then that the famous Greek Philosophers arose, but as soon as Rome assumed political leadership, they produced no philosopher worthy the name.

64. Al Khazari: Does this mean that Aristotle's philosophy is not deserving of credence.

65. The Rebbi: Certainly. He exerted his mind, because he had no tradition from any reliable source at his disposal. He meditated on the beginning and end of the world, but found as much difficulty in the theory of a beginning as in that of eternity. Finally, these abstract speculations which made for eternity, prevailed, and he found no reason to inquire into the chronology or derivation of those who lived before him. Had he lived among a people with well authenticated and generally acknowledged traditions, he would have applied his deductions and arguments to establish the theory of creation, however difficult, instead of eternity, which is even much more difficult to accept.

66. Al Khazari: Is there any decisive proof.

67. The Rebbi: Where could we find one for such a question? Heaven forbid that there should be anything in the Bible to contradict that which is manifest or proved! On the other hand, it tells of miracles and the changes of ordinary, things newly arising, or changing one into the other. This proves that the Creator of the world is able to accomplish what He will, and whenever He will. The question of eternity and creation is obscure, whilst the arguments are evenly balanced. The theory of creation derives greater weight from the prophetic tradition of Adam, Noah, and Moshe, which is more deserving of credence than mere speculation. If, after all, a believer in the Law finds himself compelled to admit an eternal matter and the existence of many worlds prior to this one, this would not impair his belief that this world was created at a certain epoch, and that Adam and Noah were the first human beings.

68. Al Khazari: Thus far I find these arguments quite satisfactory. Should we continue our conversation, I will trouble thee to adduce more decisive proofs. Now take up the thread of thy earlier exposition, how the great conviction settled in thy soul, that the Creator of body and spirit, soul, intellect and angels-He who is too high, holy and exalted for the mind still less for the senses to grasp-that He holds intercourse. with creatures made of low and contemptible material, wonderful as this may seem. For the smallest worm shows the wonders of His wisdom in a manner beyond the human mind.

69. The Rebbi: Thou hast forestalled much of my intended answer to thee. Dost, thou ascribe the wisdom apparent in the creation of an **Ant** [for example] to a sphere or star, or to any other object, to the exclusion of the Almighty Creator, who weighs and gives everything its due, giving neither too much, nor too little?

70. Al Khazari: This is ascribed to the action of Nature.

71. The Rebbi: What is Nature?

72. Al Khazari: As far as philosophy teaches, it is a certain power; only we do not know what it really is. No doubt philosophers know.

73. The Rebbi: They know as much as we do. Aristotle defined it as the beginning and primary cause through which a thing either moves or rests, not by accidents, but on account of its innate essence.

74. Al Khazari: This would mean that the thing which moves or rests on its own account has a cause through which it moves or rests. This cause is Nature.

75. The Rebbi: This opinion is the result of diligent research, criticism, and discrimination between accidental and natural occurrences. These things astonish those who hear them, but nothing else springs from the knowledge of nature.

76. Al Khazari: All I can see is, that they have misled us by these names, and caused us to place another being on a par with God, if we say that Nature is wise and active. Speaking in their sense, we might even say: possessed of intelligence.

77. The Rebbi: Certainly; but the elements, moon, sun and stars have powers such as warming, cooling, moistening, drying, etc., but do not merit that wisdom should be ascribed to them, or be reckoned more than a function. Forming, measuring, producing, however, and all that shows an intention, can only be ascribed to the All-wise and Almighty. There is no harm in calling the power which arranges matter by means of heat and cooling, **Nature**, but all intelligence must be denied it. So must the faculty of creating the embryo be denied to human beings, because they only aid matter in receiving human form from its wise Creator. Thou must not deem it improbable that exalted divine traces should be visible in this material world, when this matter is prepared to receive them. Here are to be found the roots of faith as well as of unbelief.

78. Al Khazari: How is this possible.

79. The Rebbi: These conditions which render man fit to receive this divine influence do not lie within him. It is impossible for him to gauge their quantity or quality, and even if their essence were known, yet neither their time, place, and connexion, nor suitability could be discovered. For this, inspired and detailed instruction is necessary. He who has been thus inspired, and obeys the teaching in every respect with a pure mind, is a believer. Whosoever strives by speculation and deduction to prepare the conditions for the reception of this inspiration, or by divining, as is found in the writings of astrologers, trying to call down supernatural beings, or manufacturing talismans, such a man is an unbeliever. He may bring offerings and burn incense in the name of speculation and conjecture, whilst he is in reality ignorant of that which he should do, how much, in which way, by what means, in which place, by whom, in which manner, and many other details, the enumeration of which would lead too far. He is like an ignoramus who enters the surgery of a physician famous for the curative power of his medicines. The physician is not at home, but people come for medicines. The fool dispenses them out of the jars, knowing nothing of the contents, nor how much should be given to each person. Thus, he kills with the very medicine which should have cured them. Should he by chance have effected a cure with one of the drugs, the people will turn to him and say that he helped them, till they discover that he deceived them, or they seek other advice, and cling to this without noticing that the real cure was affected by the skill of the learned physician who prepared the medicines and explained the proper manner in which they were to be administered. He also taught the patients what food and drink, exercise and rest, etc., was necessary, likewise what air was the best, and which place of repose Like unto the patients duped by the ignoramus, so were men, with few exceptions, before the time of Moshe. They were deceived by astrological and physical rules, wandered from law to law, from God to god, or adopted a plurality at the same time. They forgot their guide and master, and regarded their false gods as helping causes, whilst they are in reality damaging causes, according to their construction and arrangement. Profitable on its own account is the divine influence, hurtful on its own account the absence thereof.

80. Al Khazari: Let us now return to our subject, and explain to me how your belief grew, how it spread and became general, how opinions became united after having differed, and how long it took for the faith to lay its foundation, and to be built up into a strong and complete structure. The first element of religion appeared, no doubt, among single individuals, who supported one another in upholding the faith which it pleased God should be promulgated. Their number increases continually, they grow more powerful, or a king arises and assists them, also compels his subjects to adopt the same creed.

81. The Rebbi: In this way only rational religions, of human origin, can arise. When a man succeeds and attains an exalted position, it is said that he is supported by God, who inspired him, etc. A religion of divine origin arises suddenly. It is bidden to arise, and it is there, like the creation of the world.

82. Al Khazari: Thou surprisest me, O Rebbi.

83. The Rebbi: It is, indeed, astonishing. The Israelites lived in Egypt as slaves, six hundred thousand men above the age of twenty, descendants of the Twelve Tribes. Not one of them had separated or emigrated into another country, nor was a stranger among them. They looked forward to the promise given to their ancestors, Abraham, Itzhak, and Yaakov, that the land of Palestine should be their inheritance. At that time, it was in the power of seven mighty and prosperous nations, whilst the Israelites sighed in the depths of misery under the bondage of Pharaoh, who caused their children to be put to death, lest they should increase in number. Notwithstanding their lowly position as compared to the tyrant in his might, God sent Moshe and Aaron before Pharaoh with signs and miracles, allowing them even to change the course of nature. Pharaoh could not get away from them, nor harm them, neither could he protect himself from the ten plagues which befel the Egyptians, affecting their streams, land, air, plants, animals, bodies, even their souls. For in one moment, at midnight, died the most precious and most beloved members of their houses, viz. every firstborn male. There was no dwelling without dead, except the houses of the Israelites. All these plagues were preceded by warnings and menaces, and their cessation was notified in the same way, so that every one should become convinced that they were ordained by God, who does what He will and when He will, and were not ordinary natural phenomena, nor wrought by constellations or accident. The Israelites left the country of Pharaoh's bondage, by the command of God, the same night and at the same moment, when the firstborn died, and reached the shores of the Red Sea. They were guided by pillars of cloud and fire, and led by Moshe and Aaron, the venerated, inspired chiefs, then about eighty years of age. Up to this time they had only a few laws which they had inherited from Adam and Noah. These laws were not abrogated by Moshe, but rather increased by him. When Pharaoh pursued the Israelites, they did not have recourse to arms, being unskilled in their use. God, however, divided the sea, and they traversed it. Pharaoh and his host were drowned, and the waves washed their corpses towards the Israelites, so that they could see them with their own eyes. It is a long and well-known story.

84. Al Khazari: This is, in truth, divine power, and the commandments connected with it must be accepted. No one could imagine for a moment that this was the result of necromancy, calculation, or phantasy. For had it been possible to procure belief in any imaginary dividing of the waters, and the crossing of the same, it would also have been possible to gain credence for a similar imposition concerning their delivery from bondage, the death of their tormentors, and the capture of their goods and chattels. This would be even worse than denying the existence of God.

85. The Rebbi: And later on, when they came to the desert, which was not sown, he sent them food which, with the exception of Sabbath, was created daily for them, and they ate it for forty years.

86. Al Khazari: This also is irrefutable, viz. a thing which occurred to six hundred thousand people for forty years. Six days in the week the Manna came down, but on the Sabbath it stopped. This makes the observance of the Sabbath obligatory, since divine ordination is visible in it.

87. The Rebbi: The Sabbatical law is derived from this circumstance, as well as from the creation of the world in six days, also from another matter to be discussed later on. Although the people believed in the message of Moshe, they retained, even after the performance of the miracles, some doubt as to whether God really spake to mortals, and whether the Law was not of human origin, and only later on supported by divine inspiration. They could not associate speech with a divine being, since it is something tangible. God, however, desired to remove this doubt, and commanded them to prepare themselves morally, as well as physically, enjoining them to keep aloof from their wives, and to be ready to hear the words of God. The people prepared and became fitted to receive the divine afflatus, and even to hear publicly the words of God. This came to pass three days later, being introduced by overwhelming phenomena, lightning, thunder, earthquake and fire, which surrounded Mount Sinai. The fire remained visible on the mount forty days. They also saw

Moshe enter it and emerge from it; they distinctly heard the Ten Commandments, which represent the very essence of the Law. One of them is the ordination of Sabbath, a law which had previously been connected with the gift of the Manna. The people did not receive these ten commandments from single individuals, nor from a prophet, but from God, only they did not possess the strength of Moshe to bear the grandeur of the scene. Henceforth the people believed that Moshe held direct communication with God, that his words were not creations of his own mind, that prophecy did not as philosophers assume, burst forth in a pure soul, become united with the Active Intellect also termed Holy Spirit or Gabriel, and be then inspired. They did not believe Moshe had seen a vision in sleep, or that some one had spoken with him between sleeping and waking, so that he only heard the words in fancy, but not with his ears, that he saw a phantom, and afterwards pretended that God had spoken with him. Before such an impressive scene all ideas of jugglery vanished. The divine allocution was followed by the divine writing. For he wrote these Ten Words on two tablets of precious stone, and handed them to Moshe. The people saw the divine writing, as they had heard the divine words. Moshe made an ark by God's command, and built the Tent over it. It remained among the Israelites as long as prophecy lasted, about nine hundred years, until the people became disobedient. Then the ark was hidden, and Nebuchadnezzar conquered and drove the Israelites into exile.

88. Al Khazari: Should any one hears you relate that God spoke with your assembled multitude, and wrote tables for you, etc., he would be blamed for accusing you of holding the theory of personification You, on the other hand, are free from blame, because this grand and lofty spectacle, seen by thousands, cannot be denied. You are justified in rejecting the charge of mere reasoning and speculation.

89. The Rebbi: Heaven forbid that I should assume what is against sense and reason. The first of the Ten Commandments enjoins the belief in divine providence. The second command contains the prohibition of the worship of other gods, or the association of any being with Him, the prohibition to represent Him in statues, forms and images, or any personification of Him. How should we not deem him exalted above personification, since we do so with many of His creations, the human soul, which represents man's true essence. For that part of Moshe which spoke to us, taught and guided us, was not his tongue, or heart, or brain. Those were only organs, whilst Moshe himself is the intellectual, discriminating, incorporeal soul, not limited by place, neither too large, nor too small for any space in order to contain the images of all creatures. If we ascribe spiritual elements to it, how much more must we do so to the Creator of all? We must not, however, endeavour to reject the conclusions to be drawn from revelation. We say, then, that we do not know how the intention became corporealized and the speech evolved which struck our ear, nor what new thing God created from nought, nor what existing thing He employed. He does not lack the power. We say that He created the two tables, engraved a text on them, in the same way as He created the heaven and the stars by His will alone. God desired it, and they became concrete as He wished it, engraved with the text of the Ten Words. We also say that He divided the sea and formed it into two walls, which He caused to stand on the right and on the left of the people, for whom He made easy wide roads and a smooth ground for them to walk on without fear and trouble. This rending, constructing and arranging, are attributed to God, who required no tool or intermediary, as would be necessary for human toil. As the water stood at His command, shaped itself at His will, so the air which touched the prophet's ear, assumed the form of sounds, which conveyed the matters to be communicated by God to the prophet and the people.

90. Al Khazari: This representation is

satisfactory.

91. The Rebbi: I do not maintain that this is exactly how these things occurred; the problem is no doubt too deep for me to fathom. But the result was that every one who was present at the time became convinced that the matter proceeded from God direct. It is to be compared to the first act of creation. The belief in the law connected with those scenes is as firmly established in the mind as the belief in the creation of the world, and that He created it in the same manner in which He-as is known-created the two tablets, the manna, and other things. Thus, disappear from the soul of the believer the doubts of philosophers and materialists.

92. Al Khazari: Take care, O Rebbi, lest too great indulgence in the description of the superiority of thy people make thee not unbearable, causing thee to overlook what is known of their disobedience in spite of the revelation. I have heard that in the midst of it they made a calf and worshipped it.

93. The Rebbi: A sin which was reckoned all the heavier on account of their greatness. Great is he whose sins are counted

94. Al Khazari: This is what makes thee tedious and makes thee appear partial to thy people. What sin could be greater than this, and what deed could have exceeded this.

95. The Rebbi: Bear with me a little while that I show the lofty station of the people. For me it is sufficient that God chose them as His people from all nations of the world, and allowed His influence to rest on all of them, and that they nearly approached being addressed by Him. It even descended on their women, among whom were prophetesses, whilst since Adam only isolated individuals had been inspired till then. Adam was perfection itself, because no flaw could be found in a work of a wise and Almighty Creator, wrought from a substance chosen by Him, and fashioned according to His own design. There was no restraining influence, no fear of atavism, no question of nutrition or education during the years of childhood and growth; neither was there the influence of climate, water, or soil to consider. For He created him in the form of an adolescent, perfect in body and mind. The soul with which he was endowed was perfect; his intellect was the loftiest which it is possible for a human being to possess, and beyond this he was gifted with the divine power of such high rank, that it brought him into connexion with beings divine and spiritual, and enabled him, with slight reflection, to comprehend the great truths without instruction. We call him God's son, and we call all those who were like him also sons of God. He left many children, of whom the only one capable of taking his place was Abel, because he alone was like him. After he had been slain by Kain through jealousy of this privilege, it passed to his brother Seth, who also was like Adam, being as it were his essence and heart, whilst the others were like husks and rotten fruit. The essence of Seth, then, passed to Enosh, and in this way the divine influence was inherited by isolated individuals down to Noah. They are compared to the heart; they resembled Adam, and were styled sons of God. They were perfect outwardly and inwardly, their lives, knowledge and ability being likewise faultless. Their lives fix the chronology from Adam to Noah, as well as from Noah to Abraham. There were some, however, among them who did not come under divine influence, as Terach, but his son Abraham was the disciple of his grandfather Eber, and was born in the lifetime of Noah. Thus, the divine spirit descended from the grandfather to the grandchildren. Abraham represented the essence of Eber, being his disciple, and for this reason he was called **Ibri**. Eber represented the essence of Shem, the latter that of Noah. He inherited the temperate zone, the centre and principal part of which is Palestine, the land of prophecy. Japheth turned towards north, and Ham towards south. The essence of Abraham passed over to Itzhak, to the exclusion of the other sons who were all removed from the land, the special inheritance of Itzhak. The prerogative of Itzhak descended on Yaakov, whilst Esau was sent from the land which belonged to Yaakov. The sons of the latter were all worthy of the divine influence, as well as of the country distinguished by the divine spirit. This is the first instance of the divine influence descending on a number of people, whereas it had previously only been vouchsafed to isolated individuals. Then God tended them in Egypt, multiplied and aggrandised them, as a tree with a sound root grows until it produces perfect fruit, resembling the first fruit from which it was planted, viz. Abraham, Itzhak, Yaakov, Yosef and his brethren. The seed further produced Moshe, Aaron and Miriam, Betzalel, Oholiab, and the chiefs of the tribes, the seventy Elders, who were all endowed with the spirit of prophecy; then Yehoshua, Kaleb, Hur, and many others. Then they became worthy of having the divine light and providence made visible to them. If disobedient men existed among them, they were hated, but remained, without doubt, of the essence inasmuch as they were part of it on account of their descent and nature, and begat children who were of the same stamp. An ungodly man received consideration in proportion to the minuteness of the essence with which he was endowed, for it reappeared in his children and grandchildren according to the purity of their lineage. This is how we regard Terach and others in whom the divine afflatus was not visible, though, to a certain extent, it underlay his natural disposition, so that he begat a descendant filled with the essence, which was not the case with all the posterity of Ham and Japhet. We perceive a similar phenomenon in nature at large. Many people do not resemble their father, but take after their grand-fathers. There cannot, consequently, be any doubt that this nature and resemblance was hidden in the father, although it did not become visible outwardly, as was the nature of Eber in his children, until it reappeared in Abraham.

96. Al Khazari: This is the true greatness, which descended direct from Adam. He was the noblest creature on earth. Therefore, you rank above all the other inhabitants of the earth. But what of this privilege at the time when that sin was committed.

97. The Rebbi: All nations were given to idolatry at that time. Even had they been philosophers, discoursing on the unity and government of God, they would have been unable to dispense with images, and would have taught the masses that a divine influence hovered over this image. which was distinguished by some miraculous feature. Some of them ascribed this to God, even as we to-day treat some particular spots with reverence, going so far as to believe ourselves blessed by their dust and stones Others ascribed it to the spiritual influence of some star or constellation, or of a talisman, or to other things of that kind. The people did not pay so much attention to a single law as to a tangible image in which they believed. The Israelites had been promised that something visible would descend on them from God which they could follow, as they followed the pillars of cloud and fire when they departed from Egypt. This they pointed out, and turned to it, praising it, and worshipping God in its presence. Thus, they also turned towards the cloud which hovered over Moshe while God spake with him; they remained standing and adoring God opposite to it. Now when the people had heard the proclamation of the Ten Commandments, and Moshe had ascended the mount in order to receive the inscribed tables which he was to bring down to them, and then make an ark which was to be the point towards which they should direct their gaze during their devotions, they waited for his return clad in the same apparel in which they had witnessed the drama on Sinai, without removing their jewels or changing their clothes, remaining just as he left them, expecting every moment to see him return. He, however, tarried forty days, although he had not provided himself with food, having only left them with the intention of returning the same day. An evil spirit overpowered a portion of the people, and they began to divide into parties and factions. Many views and opinions were expressed, till at last some decided to do like the other nations, and seek an object in which they could have faith, without, however, prejudicing the supremacy of Him who had brought them out of Egypt. On the contrary, this was to be something to which they could point when relating the wonders of God, as the Philistines did with the ark when they said that God dwelt within it. We do the same with the sky and every other object concerning which we know that it is set in motion by the divine will exclusively, and not by any accident or desire of man or nature. Their sin I consisted in the manufacture of an image of a forbidden thing, and in attributing divine power to a creation of their own, something chosen by themselves without the guidance of God. Some excuse may be found for them in the dissension which had broken out among them, and in the fact that out of six hundred thousand souls the number of those who worshipped the calf was below three thousand. For those of higher station who assisted in making it an excuse might be found in the fact that they wished to clearly separate the disobedient from the pious, in order to slay those who would worship the calf. On the other hand, they sinned in causing what was only a sin of intention to become a sin in deed. This sin was not on a par with an entire lapse from all obedience to Him who had led them out of Egypt, as only one of His commands was violated by them. God had forbidden images, and in spite of this they made one. They should have waited and not have assumed power, have arranged a place of worship, an altar, and sacrifices. This had been done by the advice of the astrologers and magicians among them, who were of opinion that their actions based on their ideas would be more correct than the true ones. They resembled the fool of whom we spoke, who entered the surgery of a physician and dealt out death instead of healing to those who came there. At the same time the people did not intend to give up their allegiance to God. On the contrary, they were, in theory, more zealous in their devotion. They therefore approached Aaron, and he, desiring to make their plan public, assisted them in their undertaking. For this reason, he is to be blamed for changing their theoretical disobedience into a reality. The whole affair is repulsive to us, because in this age the majority of nations have abandoned the worship of images. It appeared less objectionable at that time, because all nations were then idolators. Had their sin consisted in constructing a house of worship of their own, and making a place of prayer, offering and veneration, the matter would not have been so grave, because nowadays we also build our houses of worship, hold them in great respect, and seek blessing through their means.

We even say that God dwells in them, and that they are surrounded by angels. If this were not essential for the gathering of our community, it would be as unknown as it was at the time of the kings, when the people were forbidden to erect places of worship, called heights. The pious kings destroyed them, lest they be venerated beside the house chosen by God in which He was to be worshipped according to His own ordinances. There was nothing strange in the form of the cherubim made by His command. In spite of these things, those who worshipped the calf were punished on the same day, and three thousand out of six hundred thousand were slain. The Manna, however, did not cease falling for their maintenance, nor the cloud to give them shade, nor the pillar of fire to guide them. Prophecy continued spreading and increasing among them, and nothing that had been granted was taken from them, except the two tables, which Moshe broke. But then he pleaded for their restoration; they were restored, and the sin was forgiven.

98. Al Khazari: The theory I had formed, and the opinion of what I saw in my dream thou now confirmest, viz. that man can only merit divine influence by acting according to God's commands and even were it not so, most men strive to obtain it, even astrologers, magicians, fire and sun worshippers, dualists etc.

99. The Rebbi: Thou art right. Our laws were written in the Torah by Moshe, who had them direct from God, and handed them down to the masses assembled in the desert. There was no necessity to quote any older authority with regard to the single chapters and verses, nor with regard to the description of sacrifices, where and in what manner they were to be offered up, and what was to be done with the blood and the limbs, etc. Everything was clearly stated by God, as the smallest matter missing would interfere with the completeness of the whole thing. It is here, as in the formations of nature, which are composed of such minute elements that they defy perception, and if their mutual relation suffered the smallest change, the whole formation would be damaged, that plant or animal, or limb, would be imperfect and nonexisting. In the same manner the law prescribes how the sacrificed animal should be dismembered, and what should be done with each limb, what should be eaten and what burnt, who should eat and who burn, and which section of priests should have the charge of offering it up, and which dared not. It also prescribed in what condition those who brought the offerings must be, so that they should be faultless, both as regards appearance and apparel, especially the High Priest, who had the privilege of entering the place of Divinity which enclosed God's glory, the ark and the Torah. To this are attached the rules for cleanliness and purity, and the various grades of purification, sanctification, and prayer, the description of which would lead us too far. In all these matters they had to rely on the reading of the Torah, combined with the traditions of the Rebbis, based on God's communications to Moshe. In the same manner the form of the Tabernacle was shown to Moshe on the mountain, viz. the tabernacle, the interior, the candlestick, the ark, and the surrounding court, with its pillars, coverings, and all appurtenances, were caused by God to appear to him in their real shape, in the form in which He commanded to have them executed. In the same way was the Temple of Shlomo built according to the model revealed to David. So also, will the last sanctuary promised us be shaped and arranged according to the details seen by the prophet Ezekiel. In the service of God there is no arguing, reasoning, and debating Had this been possible, philosophers with their wisdom and acumen would have achieved even more than Israel.

100. Al Khazari: Thus, the human mind can accept the Law cheerfully and unhesitatingly, without doubting that a prophet would come to the oppressed and enslaved people, and promise them that they would at an appointed time, thus and without delay, be delivered from bondage. Moshe led them to Palestine against seven nations, each of which was stronger than they were, assigned to each tribe its portion of the land before they reached it. All this was accomplished in the shortest space of time, and accompanied by miraculous events. This proves the omnipotence of the Sender as well as the greatness of the Messenger, and the high station of those who alone received this message. Had he said: **I was sent to guide the whole world in the right path**, and would only have partially fulfilled his task, his message would have been deficient, since the divine will would not have been carried out completely. The perfection of his work was marred by the fact that his book was written in Hebrew, which made it unintelligible to the peoples of Sind, India, and Khazar. They would, therefore, be unable to practise his laws till some centuries had elapsed, or they had been prepared for it by changes of conquest, or alliance, but not through the revelation of that prophet himself, or of another who would stand up for him, and testify to his law.

101. The Rebbi: Moshe invited only his people and those of his own tongue to accept his law, whilst God promised that there should at all times be prophets to expound his law. This He did so long as they found favour in His sight, and His presence was with them.

102. Al Khazari: Would it not have been better or more commensurate with divine wisdom, if all mankind had been guided in the true path.

103. The Rebbi: Or would it not have been best for all animals to have been reasonable beings? Thou hast, apparently, forgotten what we said previously concerning the genealogy of Adam's progeny, and how the spirit of divine prophecy rested on one person, who was chosen from his brethren, and the essence of his father. It was he in whom this divine light was concentrated. He was the kernel, whilst the others were as shells which had no share in it. The sons of Yaakov were, however, distinguished from other people by godly qualities, which made them, so to speak, an angelic caste. Each of them, being permeated by the divine essence, endeavoured to attain the degree of prophecy, and most of them succeeded in so doing. Those who were not successful strove to approach it by means of pious acts, sanctity, purity, and intercourse with prophets. Know that he who converses with a prophet experiences spiritualization during the time he listens to his oration. He differs from his own kind in the purity of soul, in a yearning for the higher degrees and attachment to the qualities of meekness and purity. This was a manifest proof to them, and a clear and convincing sign of reward hereafter. For the only result to be expected from this is that the human soul becomes divine, being detached from material senses, joining the highest world, and enjoying the vision of the divine light, and hearing the divine speech. Such a soul is safe from death, even after its physical organs have perished. If thou, then, findest a religion the knowledge and practice of which assists in the attainment of this degree, at the place pointed out and with the conditions laid down by it, this is beyond doubt the religion which insures the immortality of the soul after the demise of the body.

104. Al Khazari: The anticipations of other churches are grosser and more sensuous than yours.

105. The Rebbi: They are none of them realized till after death, whilst during this life nothing points to them.

106. Al Khazari: May be; I have never seen any one who believed in these promises desire their speedy fulfilment. On the contrary, if he could delay them a thousand years, and remain in the bonds of this life in spite of the hardship of this world, he would prefer it.

107. The Rebbi: What is thy opinion concerning him who witnessed those grand and divine scenes.

108. Al Khazari: That he, no doubt, longs for the perpetual separation of his soul from his material senses, in order to enjoy that light. It is such a person who would desire death.

109. The Rebbi: Now all that our promises imply is that we shall become connected with the divine influence by means of prophecy, or something nearly approaching it, and also through our relation to the divine influence, as displayed to us in grand and awe-inspiring miracles. Therefore, we do not find in the Bible: 'If you keep this law, I will bring you after death into beautiful gardens and great pleasures.' On the contrary it is said: 'You shall be my chosen people, and I will be a God unto you, who will guide you. Whoever of you comes to me, and ascends to heaven, is as those who, themselves, dwell among the angels, and my angels shall dwell among them on earth. You shall see them singly or in hosts, watching you and fighting for you without your joining in the fight. You shall remain in the country which forms a stepping-stone to this degree, viz. the Holy Land. Its fertility or barrenness, its happiness or misfortune, depend upon the divine influence which your conduct will merit, whilst the rest of the world would continue its natural course. For if the divine presence is among you, you will perceive by the fertility of your country, by the regularity with which your rainfalls appear in their due seasons, by your victories over your enemies in spite of your inferior numbers, that your affairs are not managed by simple laws of nature, but by the divine Will. You also see that drought, death, and wild beasts pursue you as a result of disobedience, although the whole world lives in peace. This shows you that your concerns are arranged by a higher power than mere nature.' All this, the laws included, is closely connected with the promises, and no disappointment is feared. All these promises have one basis, viz. the anticipation of being near God and His hosts. He who attains this degree need not fear death, as is clearly demonstrated in our Law. The following parable will illustrate this: One of a company of friends who sought solicitude in a remote spot, once journeyed to India, and had honour and rank bestowed on him by her king, who knew that he was one of these friends, and who had also known their fathers, former comrades of his own. The king loaded him with presents for his friends, gave him costly raiment for himself, and then dismissed him, sending members of his own retinue to accompany him on his return journey. No one knew that they belonged to the court, nor that they travelled into the desert. He had received commissions and treaties, and in return he had to swear fealty to the king. Then he and his Indian escort returned to his companions, and received a hearty welcome from them. They took pains to accommodate them and to show them honour. They also built a castle and allowed them to dwell in it. Henceforth they frequently sent ambassadors to India to wait upon the king, which was now easier of accomplishment, as the first messengers guided them the shortest and straightest route. All knew that travelling in that country was rendered easier by swearing allegiance to his king and respecting his ambassadors. There was no occasion to inquire why this homage was necessary, because it was patent that by this means he came into connexion with the monarch-a most pleasing circumstance. Now these companions are the Children of Israel, the first traveller is Moshe, the later travellers are the prophets, whilst the Indian messengers are the Shekinah and the angels. The precious garments are the spiritual light which dwelt in the soul of Moshe on account of his prophet ship, whilst the visible light appeared on his countenance. The presents are the two tables with the Ten Commandments. Those in possession of other laws saw nothing of this, but were told: 'Continue in obedience to the King of India as this company of friends, and you will after death become the associates of the king, otherwise he will turn you away, and punish you after death.' Some might say: No one ever returned to inform us whether, after death, he dwelt in paradise or in hell. The majority were satisfied with the arrangement, which coincided with their views. They obeyed willingly, and allowed themselves to entertain a faint hope, which to all appearance was a very strong one, as they commenced to be proud and to behave haughtily towards other people. But how can they boast of expectations after death to those who enjoy the fulfilment already in life? Is not the nature of the prophets and godly men nearer to immortality than the nature of him who never reached that degree.

110. Al Khazari: It does not agree with common sense that when man perishes, body and soul should disappear at the same time, as is the case with animals, and that the philosophers alone will-as they believe-escape. The same applies to the statement made by believers in other faiths-that man, by the pronunciation of one word alone, may inherit paradise, even if, during the whole of his life, he knew no other word than this, and of this did not even understand the great significance, viz. that one word raised him from the ranks of a brute to that of an angel. He who did not utter this word would remain an animal, though he might be a learned and pious philosopher, who yearned for God all his life.

111. The Rebbi: We do not deny that the good actions of any man, to whichever people he may belong, will be rewarded by God. But the priority belongs to people who are near God during their life, and we estimate the rank they occupy near God after death accordingly.

112. Al Khazari: Apply this also in the other direction, and judge their degree in the next world according to their station in this world.

113. The Rebbi: I see thee reproaching us with our degradation and poverty, but the best of other religions boasts of both. Do they not glorify Him who said: He who smites thee on the right cheek, turn to him the left also; and he who takes away thy coat, let him have thy shirt also. He and his friends and followers, after hundreds of years of contumely, flogging and slaying, attained their well-known success, and just in these things they glorify. This is also the history of the founder of Islam and his friends, who eventually prevailed, and became powerful. The nations boast of these, but not of these kings whose power and might are great, whose walls are strong, and whose chariots are terrible. Yet our relation to God is a closer one than if we had reached greatness already on earth.

114. Al Khazari: This might be so, if your humility were voluntary; but it is involuntary, and if you had power you would slay.

115. The Rebbi: Thou hast touched our weak spot, O King of the Khazars. If the majority of us, as thou sayest, would learn humility towards God and His law from our low station, Providence would not have forced us to bear it for such a long period. Only 'the smallest portion thinks thus. Yet the majority may expect a reward, because they bear their degradation partly from necessity, partly of their own free will. For whoever wishes to do so can become the friend and equal of his oppressor by uttering one word, and without any difficulty. Such conduct does not escape the just Judge. If we bear our exile and degradation for God's sake, as is meet, we shall be the pride of the generation which will come with the MASHIACH, and accelerate the day of the deliverance we hope for. Now we do not allow any one who embraces our religion theoretically by means of a word alone to take equal rank with ourselves, but demand actual self-sacrifice, purity, knowledge, circumcision, and numerous religious ceremonies. The convert must adopt our mode of life entirely. We must bear in mind that the rite of circumcision is a divine symbol, ordained by God to indicate that our desires should be curbed, and discretion used, so that what we engender may be fitted to receive the divine Influence. God allows him who treads this path, as well as his progeny, to approach Him very closely. Those, however, who become Jews do not take equal rank with born Israelites, who are specially privileged to attain to prophecy, whilst the former can only achieve something by learning from them, and can only become pious and learned, but never prophets.

Kuzari — First Essay

As regards the promises at which thou art so astonished, our sages, long ago, gave descriptions of paradise and hell, their length and width, and depicted the enjoyments and punishments in greater detail than is given in any later religions. From the very beginning I only spoke to thee of what is contained in the books of the Prophets They, however, do not discuss the promises of after-life with so much diffuseness as is done in the sayings of the Rebbis. Nevertheless, the prophetic books allude to the return of the dust of the human body to the earth, whilst the spirit returns to the Creator who gave it. They also mention the resurrection of the dead at some future time, the sending of a prophet called Eliyahu AlKhidr, who had already been sent once, but who was taken away by God in the same way as another said that he never tasted death. The Torah contains the prayer of one who was specially privileged to become a prophet, and he prayed that his death might be made easy, and his end be as the end of the Children of Israel. After the death of Samuel King Saul invoked his aid, and he prophesied for him concerning all that would happen to him in the same way as he had prophesied to him whilst living. Although this action of Saul, viz. consulting the dead, is forbidden in our law, it shows that the people at the time of the prophets believed in the immortality of the soul after the decay of the body. For this reason, they consulted the dead.

All educated people, including women, know by heart the opening prayer of our morning liturgy, which runs as follows: O Lord, the spirit which Thou hast breathed into me is hallowed; Thou hast created it, thou guardest it, and Thou wilt after a time take it from me, but wilt restore it to me in the other world. As long as it is within me, I praise Thee, and am grateful to Thee, O Lord of the universe. Praise be to Thee who restoreth the spirit unto the dead. The notion of 'Paradise' itself, of which people often speak, is derived from the Torah, being the exalted abode, which was intended for Adam. Had he not been disobedient, he would have remained in it for ever. Similarly, **Gehinnom** [Hell] was nothing but a well-known place near the Holy House, a trench in which the fire was never extinguished, because unclean bones, carrion and other impurities used to be burned there. The word is a compound Hebrew one.

116. Al Khazari: If that is so, then there has been nothing new since your religion was promulgated, except certain details concerning paradise and hell, their arrangement, and the repetition and enlargement of these.

117. The Rebbi: Even this is not new either. The Rebbis have said so much on the subject that there is nothing thou couldst hear concerning it which could not be found in their writings, if thou didst but search for it.

Kuzari — First Essay

Second Essay

1. After this the Khazari, as is related in the history of the Khazars, was anxious to reveal to his **Vezier** [Minister] in the mountains of Warsan the secret of his dream and its repetition, in which he was urged to seek the God-pleasing deed. The king and his Vezier travelled to the deserted mountains on the sea shore, and arrived one night at the cave in which some Jews used to celebrate the Sabbath. They disclosed their identity to them, embraced their religion, were circumcised in the cave, and then returned to their country, eager to learn the Jewish law. They kept their conversion secret, however, until they found an opportunity of disclosing the fact gradually to a few of their special friends. When the number had increased, they made the affair public, and induced the rest of the Khazars to embrace the Jewish faith. They sent to various countries for scholars and books, and studied the Torah. Their chronicles also tell of their prosperity, how they beat their foes, conquered their lands, secured great treasures; how their army swelled to hundreds of thousands, how they loved their faith, and fostered such love for the Holy House that they erected a Tabernacle in the shape of that built by Moshe. They also honoured and cherished those born Israelites who lived among them. While the king studied the Torah and the books of the prophets, he employed the Rebbi as his teacher, and put many questions to him on Hebrew matters. The first of these questions referred to the names and attributes ascribed to God and their anthropomorphistic forms, which are unmistakeably objectionable alike both to reason and to law.

2. Said the Rebbi: All names of God, save the Tetragrammaton, are predicates and attributive descriptions, derived from the way His creatures are affected by His decrees and measures. He is called merciful, if he improves the condition of any man whom people pity for his sorry plight. They attribute to Him mercy and compassion, although this is, in our conception, surely nothing but a weakness of the soul and a quick movement of nature. This cannot be applied to God, who is a just Judge, ordaining the poverty of one individual and the wealth of another. His nature remains quite unaffected by it. He has no sympathy with one, nor anger against another. We see the same in human judges to whom questions are put. They decide according to law, making some people happy, and others miserable. He appears to us, as we observe His doings, sometimes a merciful and compassionate God, sometimes. a jealous and revengeful God, whilst He never changes from one attribute to the other. All attributes excepting the Tetragrammaton are divided into three classes, viz. creative, relative and negative. As regards the creative attributes, they are derived from acts emanating from Him by ways of natural medium, making poor and rich, exalting or casting down, 'merciful and compassionate,' 'jealous and revengeful,' 'strong and almighty,' and the like. As regards the relative attributes, viz. 'Blessed, praised, glorified, holy, exalted, and extolled,' they are borrowed from the reverence given to Him by mankind. However numerous these may be, they produce no plurality, as far as He is concerned, nor do they affect his Unity. As regards the negative attributes, such as 'Living, Only, First and Last,' they are given to Him in order to negative their contrasts, but not to establish them in the sense we understand them. For we cannot understand life except accompanied by sensibility and movement. God, however, is above them. We describe Him as living in order to negative the idea of the rigid and dead, since it would be an a priori conclusion that that which does not live is dead. This cannot, however, be applied to the intellect. One cannot, speak of time as being endowed with life, yet it does not follow that it is dead, since its nature has nothing to do with either life or death. In the same way one cannot call a stone ignorant, although we may say that it is not learned. Just as a stone is too low to be brought into connexion with learning or ignorance, thus the essence of God is too exalted to have anything to do with life or death, nor can the terms light or darkness be applied to it. If we were asked whether this essence is light or darkness, we should say light by way of metaphor, for fear one might conclude that that which is not light must be darkness. As a matter of fact we must say that only material bodies are subject to light and darkness, but the divine essence is no body, and can consequently only receive the attributes of light or darkness by way of simile, or in order to negative an attribute hinting at a deficiency. Life and death are, therefore, only applicable to material bodies, whilst the divine essence is as much exempt from both as it is highly extolled above them. The 'life' of which we speak in this connexion is not like ours, and this is what I wish to state, since 'we cannot think of any other kind of life but ours. It is as if one would say: We know not what it is. If we say - living God' and 'God of life, it is but a relative expression placed in opposition to the gods of the Gentiles, which are 'dead gods' from which no action emanates. In the same way we take the term One, viz. to negative plurality, but not to establish unity as we understand it. For we call a thing one, when the component parts are coherent and of the same materials, one bone, one sinew, one water, one air. In a similar way time is compared to a compact body, and we speak of one day, and one year. The divine essence is exempt from complexity and divisibility, and 'one' only stands to exclude plurality. In the same way we style Him **First** in order to exclude the notion of any later origin, but not to assert that He has a beginning; thus, also **Last** stands to repudiate the idea that His existence has no end, but not to fix a term for Him. All these attributes neither touch on the divine essence, nor do they lead us to assume a multiplicity. The attributes which are connected with the Tetragrammaton are those which describe His power of creating without any natural intermediaries, viz. Creator, Producer, Maker, To Him who alone doeth great wonders, which means that He creates by His bare intention and will, to the exclusion of any assisting cause. This is perhaps meant in the word of the Torah: And I appeared unto Abraham… as El Shaddai, viz. in the way of power and dominion, as is said: He suffered no man to do them wrong; yea, He reproved kings for their sake. He did not, however, perform any miracle for the patriarchs as He did for Moshe, saying: but my name **Y H W H** was I not known to them. This means by My name **Y H W H**, since the beth in beel shaddai refers to the former. The wonders done for Moshe and the Israelites left no manner of doubt in their souls that the Creator of the world also created these things which He brought into existence immediately by His will, as the plagues of Egypt, the dividing of the Red Sea, the manna, the pillar of a cloud, and the like. The reason of this was not because they were higher than the Patriarchs, but because they were a multitude, and had nourished doubt in their souls, whilst the patriarchs had fostered the utmost faith and purity of mind. If they had all their lives been pursued by misfortune, their faith in God would not have suffered. Therefore, they required no signs. We also style Him wise of heart, because He is the essence of intelligence, and intelligence itself; but this is no attribute. As to **Almighty**, this belongs to the creative attributes.

3. Al Khazari: How dost thou explain those attributes which are even of a more corporeal nature than those, viz. seeing, hearing, speaking, writing the tablets, descending on mount Sinai, rejoicing in His works, grieved in His heart.

4. The Rebbi: Did I not compare him with a just judge in whose qualities no change exists, and from whose decrees result the prosperity and good fortune of people, so that they say that he loves them and takes pleasure in them? Others, whose fate it is to have their houses destroyed and themselves be annihilated, would describe Him as filled with hate and wrath. Nothing, however, that is done or spoken escapes Him, He sees and hears; the air and all bodies came into existence by His will, and assumed shape by His command, as did heaven and earth. He is also described as 'speaking and writing.' Similarly, from the aethereal and spiritual substance, which is called **holy spirit**, arose the spiritual forms called **glory of God**. Metaphorically He is called **Y H W H**. who descended on the mount Sinai. We shall discuss this more minutely when treating on metaphysics.

5. Al Khazari: Granting that thou hast justified the use of these attributes, so that no idea of plurality needs of necessity follow, yet a difficulty remains as regards the attribute of Will with which thou dost invest Him, but which the philosopher denies.

6. The Rebbi: If no other objection is raised, except the Will, we will soon vindicate ourselves. We say: O philosophers, what is it which in thy opinion made the heavens revolve continually, the uppermost sphere carrying the whole, without place or inclination in its movement, the earth firmly fixed in the centre without support or prop; which fashioned the order of the universe in quantity, quality, and the forms we perceive? Thou canst not help admitting this, for things did neither create themselves nor each other. Now the same adapted the air to giving the sound of the Ten Commandments, and formed the writing engraved in the tables, call it will, or thing, or what thou wilt.

7. Al Khazari: The secret of the attributes is now clear, and I understand the meaning of **The Glory of God**, and **Angel of God**, and **Shekhinah** [God's presence]. They are names applied by the prophets to things perceptible, as **Pillar of Cloud**, and **Consuming Fire**, Cloud, Mist, Fire, Splendour, as it is said of the light in the morning, in the evening, and on cloudy days that the rays of light go forth from the sun, although it is not visible. Yet we say that the rays of light are inseparable from the sun, although in reality this is not so. It is the terrestrial bodies which, being opposite to it, are affected by it, and reflect its light.

8. The Rebbi: Even so does the glory of God, which is only a ray of the divine light, benefit His people in His country.

9. Al Khazari: I understand what thou meanest by **His people**, but less intelligible is what thou sayest about **His country**.

10. The Rebbi: Thou wilt have no difficulty in perceiving that one country may have higher qualifications than others. There are places in which particular plants, metals, or animals are found, or where the inhabitants are distinguished by their form and character, since perfection or deficiency of the soul are produced by the mingling of the elements.

11. Al Khazari: Yet I never heard that the inhabitants of Palestine were better than other people.

12. The Rebbi: How about the hill on which you say that the vines thrive so well? If it had not been properly planted and cultivated, it would never produce grapes. Priority belongs, in the first instance, to the people which, as stated before, is the essence and kernel of the nations. In the second instance, it would belong to the country, on account of the religious acts connected with it, which I would compare to the cultivation of the vineyard. No other place would share the distinction of the divine influence, just as no other mountain might be able to produce good wine.

13. Al Khazari: How could this be? In the time between Adam and Moshe were not prophetic visions in other places granted to Abraham in Ur of the Chaldaeans, Ezekiel and Daniel at Babylon, and Jeremiah in Egypt.

14. The Rebbi: Whosoever prophesied did so either in the Holy Land, or concerning it, viz. Abraham in order to reach it, Ezekiel and Daniel on account of it. The two latter had lived during the time of the first Temple, had seen the Shekhinah, through the influence of which each one who was duly prepared became of the elect, and able to prophesy. Adam lived and died in the land. Tradition tells us that in the cave of Machpelah were buried the four pairs: Adam and Eve, Abraham and Sarah, Itzhak and Rebecca, Yaakov and Leah. This is the land which bore the name **before the Lord**, and of which it is stated that - **The eyes of the Lord thy God are always upon it**. It was also the first object of jealousy and envy between Cain and Abel, when they desired to know which of them would be Adam's successor, and heir to his essence and intrinsic perfection; to inherit the land, and to stand in connexion with the divine influence, whilst the other would be a nonentity. Then Abel was killed by Cain, and the realm was without an heir. It is stated that **Cain** went out of the presence of Lord, which means that he left the land, saying: Behold, thou hast driven me out this day from the face of the earth, and from Thy face shall I be hid. In the same way is it said: But Yonah rose up to flee unto Tarshish from the presence of the Lord, but he only fled from the place of prophecy. God, however, brought him back there out of the belly of the fish, and appointed him prophet in the land. When Seth was born, he was like Adam, as it is said: He begat in his own likeness, after his image, and took Abel's place, as it is said: For God has appointed me another seed, instead of Abel, whom Cain slew. He merited the title: Son of God, like Adam, and he had a claim on the land, which is the next step to paradise. The land was then the object of jealousy between Itzhak and Ishmael, till the latter was rejected as worthless, although it was said concerning him: Behold, I have blessed him, and will multiply him exceedingly, in worldly prosperity; but immediately after it is said: My covenant will I establish with Itzhak, which refers to his connexion with the divine influence and happiness in the world to come. Neither Ishmael nor Esau could boast of a covenant, although they were otherwise prosperous. Jealousy arose between Yaakov and Esau for the birthright and blessing, but Esau was rejected in favour of Yaakov, in spite of his strength and the latter's weakness. Jeremiah's prophecy concerning Egypt was uttered in Egypt itself. This was also the case with Moshe, Aaron and Miriam. Sinai and **Paran** are reckoned as belonging to Palestine, because they are on this side of the Red Sea, as it is said: 'And I will set thy bounds from the Red Sea, even unto the sea of the Philistines, and from the desert unto the river. The **desert** is that of Parun, that great and terrible wilderness, being the southern border. The fourth river is Euphrates, designates the northern border, where there were the altars of the Patriarchs, who were answered by fire from heaven and the divine light. The **binding** of Itzhak took place on a desolate mountain, viz. Moriah. Not till the days of David, when it was inhabited, was the secret revealed that it was the place specially prepared for the Shekhinah. Araunah, the Jebusite, tilled his land there. Thus, it is said: And Abraham called the name of the place, The Lord shall see, as it is said to this day, in the mount of the Lord it shall be seen. In the Book of the Chronicles, it is stated more clearly that the Temple was built on mount Moriah. These are, without doubt, the places worthy of being called the gates of heaven. Dost thou not see that Yaakov ascribed the vision which he saw, not to the purity of his soul, nor to his belief, nor to true integrity, but to the place, as it is said: How awful is this place. Prior to this it is said: And he lighted upon a certain place, viz. the chosen one. Was not Abraham also, and after having been greatly exalted, brought into contact with the divine influence, and made the heart of this essence, removed from his country to the place in which his perfection should become complete. Thus, the agriculturer finds the root of a good tree in a desert place. He transplants it into properly tilled ground, to improve it and make it grow; to change it from a wild root into a cultivated one, from one which bore fruit by chance only to one which produced a luxuriant crop. In the same way the gift of prophecy was retained among Abraham's descendants in Palestine, the property of many as long as they remained in the land, and fulfilled the required conditions, viz. purity, worship, and sacrifices, and, above all, the reverence of the Shekhinah.

For the divine influence, one might say, singles out him who appears worthy of being connected with it, such as prophets and pious men, and is their God. Reason chooses those whose natural gifts are perfect, viz. Philosophers and those whose souls and character are so harmonious that it can find its dwelling among them. The spirit of life, pure and simple, is to be found in beings which are endowed with ordinary primary faculties, and particularly adapted to higher vitality-viz. animals. Finally, organic life finds its habitat in a mixture of harmonious elements, and produces-plant.

15. Al Khazari: These are the general rules of a science which must be classified. This does not concern us now, and I will ask thee about it when we speak on the' subject. Continue thy discourse on the special advantages of the Land of Israel.

16. The Rebbi: It was appointed to guide the world, and apportioned to the tribes of Israel from the time of the confusion of languages, as it is said: When the Highest divided among the nations their inheritance. Abraham was not fit to gain the divine influence, and to enter into a mutual compact, until he had, in Palestine, made the covenant with Him 'between the pieces. What is now thy opinion of a select community which has merited the appellation

people of God, and also a special name called **the inheritance of God**, and of seasons fixed by Him, not merely agreed upon or settled by astronomical calculations, and therefore styled "Sabbath of the land" **feasts of the Lord**. The rules regarding purity and worship, prayers and performances, are fixed by God, and therefore called work of God and service of the Lord.

17. Al Khazari: In such an arrangement the glory of God was bound to become apparent.

18. The Rebbi: Dost thou not see that even the land was given its Sabbaths, as it is said: Sabbath of the land, and the land shall keep a Sabbath unto the Lord. It is forbidden to sell it for ever, as it is said: For Mine is the land. Observe that the feasts of the Lord, and the Sabbaths of the land, belong to the land of the Lord.

19. Al Khazari: Was not the day primarily calculated as dawning first in China, because it forms the eastern commencement of the inhabited earth.

20. The Rebbi: The beginning of the Sabbath must be calculated from Sinai, or rather Alush, where the Mannah first descended. Consequently, Sabbath does not come in till the sun has set behind Sinai, and so on to the remote west, and round the globe to China, which is the extreme end of the inhabited earth. Sabbath begins in China eighteen hours later than in Palestine, since the latter lies in the centre of the world. Sunset in Palestine, therefore, concurs with midnight in China, and midday in Palestine concurs with sunset in China. This is the problem of the system based on the eighteen hours in the Talmudical rule: If the conjunction of the moon takes place before midday, the new moon becomes visible near sunset. This refers to Palestine, the place where the law was given, and where Adam at the end of Sabbath was transferred from paradise. It is there where the calendar began after the six days of creation. Adam, then, began to name the days, as he did with all that dwelt on earth, and the following generations continued counting in the same way. This is the reason why there is no difference among mankind about the seven days of the week, which commenced at the hour when the inhabitants of the extreme west held noon. This was the hour of sunset for Palestine, and at this moment the first light was created, the sun being created later on. This first light was but an illumination, which soon passed away, leaving the world in darkness. The established order was then that night preceded day, as it is written: 'It was evening and it was morning.' In the same manner the Torah ordained: From evening unto evening. Do not quote against me those recent astronomers, the thieves of science, though their theft was unintentional. They found, however, their science in a precarious condition, since the eye of prophecy was stricken with blindness; so, they had recourse to speculation, and composed books on the strength of it. In contradistinction to the Torah, they considered China as the original home of the calculation of the days. The contrast is not, however, complete, because they agree with the Jewish theory in assuming the beginning of the break of the day to have taken place in China. The difference between our theory and theirs consists chiefly in the circumstance that we count the night before the day. The 'eighteen' hours must, consequently, be made the basis of the nomination of the days of the week. For there are six hours between Palestine, where the nomination of the days began, and the place of the sun at the time when nomination began. Thus, the name of Sabbath, was employed for the beginning of the day on which the sun rose for the extreme west, whilst it set for Adam in Palestine. It kept the name 'beginning of Sabbath' till the sun culminated for him eighteen hours later, when it was evening in China, and also beginning of the Sabbath. This was the extreme limit for the day to be called Sabbath, because the region further on is only called east of the place where the days began to be counted. A place must, however, exist which is at the same time extreme west and the beginning of east. This is, for Palestine, the beginning of the inhabited world, not only from the point of view of the law, but also from that of natural science. For it would be impossible for the days of the week to have the same names all over the world unless we fix one place which marks the beginning, and another one not far off, not that the one be merely an eastern point for the other, but that the one should be east absolute, and the other west absolute. If this were not so the days could not have definite names, since every point of the equator can be east or west at the same time. China would thus be east for Palestine, but west for the antipodal side. The latter would be east for China, but west for what we call west, and the last-named would be east for the antipodal side, but west for Palestine, and there would be neither east, nor west, nor beginning, nor end, nor definite names for the days. Adam, however, did give definite names to the days, taking Palestine for his starting-point, but each name spreads over a certain geographical latitude, because it is impossible to fix the horizon for every single point on earth Jerusalem itself would have many east and west points; the east of Zion would not be also the east of the Temple, and their horizons, strictly speaking, different, though not noticeable to the eye. This would be the case in a greater degree between Damascus and Jerusalem, and we could not deny that in the former place Sabbath commenced earlier than it does in the latter, and in Jerusalem sooner than it does in Egypt. A certain latitude must, therefore, be allowed. But the latitude in which differences in the nomination of the day become apparent amounts to eighteen hours, neither more nor less. The inhabitants of one meridian still call the day Sabbath, whilst those of another are past it, and so on till eighteen hours after the time when the Sabbath began, and the sun culminated in Jerusalem. It is then when the name Sabbath comes to an end. Therefore no one exists who would call the day Sabbath, but uses the name of the next day. This is meant by the words: If the conjunction takes place before noon, it is understood that the new moon is visible at sunset. In other words: If the Molad takes place before noon on the Sabbath in Yerusalem, it is understood that the new moon is visible on the Sabbath at sunset. This is because the name Sabbath is retained for eighteen hours after the reason for so calling it had departed from the place where it had begun, and the sun a day and a night later culminates again in Palestine. The new moon is, therefore, bound to appear at the eastern border of China in the twilight of the Sabbath. This agrees with the rule of the sages: A night and a day are reckoned to the month. The name Sabbath gives place everywhere to Sunday, although Palestine had before that left Sabbath, and was in the midst of Sunday. The intention of this rule was that the name of the same day of the week should hold good all over the world, and the question could be put both to the inhabitants of China and the West: On which day did you celebrate the New Year. The answer would be: **On Sabbath**. This notwithstanding that the latter people had finished the feast, whilst the former, according to the geographical position of their country towards Palestine, were still celebrating it. With regard to the name of the days of the week, they had both kept the same day. Thus does the knowledge of the 'Sabbath of the Lord' and the Festivals of the Lord, depend upon the land which is the inheritance of the Lord, and has, as thou didst read, the other names of His holy mountain, His footstool, Gate of heaven. For the law shall go forth from Zion. Thou didst also read how the Patriarchs endeavoured to live in the country whilst it was in the hands of the pagans, how they yearned for it, and had their bones carried into it, as did Yaakov and Joseph. Moshe prayed to see it, and when this was denied to him, he considered it a misfortune. Thereupon it was shown to him from the summit of Pisgah, which was to him an act of grace. Persians, Indians, Greeks, and children of other nations begged to be allowed to offer up sacrifices, and to be prayed for in the holy Temple; they spent their wealth at the place, though they believed in other laws not recognized by the Torah. They honour it to this day, although the **Shekhinah** no longer appears there. All nations make pilgrimages to it, long for it, excepting we ourselves, because we are punished and in disgrace. All the Rebbis tell of its great qualities would take too long to relate.

21. Al Khazari: Let me hear a few of their observations.

22. The Rebbi: One sentence is: All roads lead up to Palestine, but none from it. Concerning a woman who refuses to go there with her husband, they decreed that she is divorced, and forfeits her marriage settlement. On the other hand, if the husband refuses to accompany his wife to Palestine, he is bound to divorce her and pay her settlement. They further say: It is better to dwell in the Holy Land, even in a town mostly inhabited by heathens, than abroad in a town chiefly peopled by Israelites; for he who dwells in the Holy Land is compared to him who has a God, whilst he who dwells abroad is compared to him who has no God. Thus says David: For they have driven me out this day from abiding in the inheritance of the Lord, saying, Go, serve other gods, which means that he who dwells abroad is as if he served strange gods. To Egypt they ascribed a certain superiority over other countries on the basis of a syllogism in the following way: If Egypt, with regard to which a covenant was made, is a forbidden land, other countries are still more so. Another saying is: To be buried in Palestine is as if buried beneath the altar. They praise him who is in the land more than him who is carried thither dead. This is expressed thus: He who embraces it when alive is not like him who does so after his death. They say concerning him who could live there, but did not do so, and only ordered his body to be carried thither after his death: While you lived you made Mine inheritance an abomination, but in death - you come and contaminate my country. It is told that Rebbi Hananyah, when asked whether it was lawful for a person to go abroad in order to marry the widow of his brother, said: His brother married a pagan woman; praised be God who caused him to die; now this one follows him the sages also forbade selling estates or the remains of a house to a heathen, or leaving a house in ruins. Other sayings are: Fines can only be imposed in the land itself; no slave must be transported abroad, and many similar regulations. Further, the atmosphere of the Holy Land makes wise. They expressed their love of the land as follows: He who walks four yards in the land is assured of happiness in the world to come, Rebbi Zera said to a heathen who criticized his foolhardiness in crossing a river without waiting to reach a ford, in his eagerness to enter the land: How can the place which Moshe and Aaron could not reach, be reached by me.

23. Al Khazari: If this be so, thou fallest short of the duty laid down in thy law, by not endeavouring to reach that place, and making it thy abode in life and death, although thou sayest: Have mercy on Zion, for it is the house of our life, and believest that the Shekhinah will return thither. And had it no other preference than that the Shekhinah dwelt there five hundred years, this is sufficient reason for men's souls to retire thither and find purification there, as happens near the abodes of the pious and the prophets. Is it not 'the gate of heaven. All nations agree on this point. Christians believe that the souls are gathered there and then lifted up to heaven. Islam teaches that it is the place of the ascent, and that prophets are caused to ascend from there to heaven, and, further, that it is the place of gathering on the day of Resurrection. Everybody turns to it in prayer and visits it in pilgrimage. Thy bowing and kneeling in the direction of it is either mere appearance or thoughtless worship. Yet your first forefathers chose it as an abode in preference to their birthplaces, and lived there as strangers, rather than as citizens in their own country. This they did even at a time when the Shekhinah was yet visible, but the country was full of unchastity, impurity, and idolatry. Your fathers, however, had no other desire than to remain in it. Neither did they leave it in times of dearth and famine except by God's permission. Finally, they directed their bones to be buried there.

24. The Rebbi: This is a severe reproach, O king of the Khazars. It is the sin which kept the divine promise with regard to the second Temple, viz.: Sing and rejoice, O daughter of Zion, from being fulfilled. Divine Providence was ready to restore everything as it had been at first, if they had all willingly consented to return. But only a part was ready to do so, whilst the majority and the aristocracy remained in Babylon, preferring dependence and slavery, and unwilling to leave their houses and their affairs. An allusion to them might be found in the enigmatic words of Shlomo: I sleep, but my heart waketh. He designates the exile by sleep, and the continuance of prophecy among them by the wakefulness of the heart. It is the voice of my beloved that knocketh means God's call to return; My head is filled with dew alludes to the Shekhinah which emerged from the shadow of the Temple. The words: 'I have put off my coat,' refer to the people's slothfulness in consenting to return. The sentence: 'My beloved stretcheth forth his hand through the opening' may be interpreted as the urgent call of Ezra, Nehemiah, and the Prophets, until a portion of the people grudgingly responded to their invitation. In accordance with their mean mind, they did not receive full measure. Divine Providence only gives man as much as he is prepared to receive;

if his receptive capacity be small, he obtains little, and much if it be great. Were we prepared to meet the God of our forefathers with a pure mind, we should find the same salvation as our fathers did in Egypt. If we say: Worship his holy hill-worship at His Footstool-He who restoreth His glory to Zion. and other words, this is but as the chattering of the starling and the nightingale. We do not realise what we say by this sentence, nor others, as thou rightly observest, O Prince of the Khazars.

25. Al Khazari: Enough on this subject. Now I should like an explanation of what I read about the sacrifices. Reason cannot accept such expressions as: My offering, My bread for My sacrifices made by fire, for a sweet savour unto Me, employed in connexion with the sacrifices, describing them as being God's offering, bread, and incense.

26. The Rebbi: The expression: By My fires removes all difficulty. It states that offering, bread and sweet savour, which are ascribed to Me, in reality belong to My fires, to the fire which was kindled at God's behest, and fed by the offerings. The remaining pieces were food for the priests. The deeper signification of this was to create a well-arranged system, upon which the King should rest in an exalted, but not local sense. As a symbol of the Divine Influence, consider the reasoning soul which dwells in the perishable body. If its physical and nobler faculties are properly distributed and arranged, raising it high above the animal world, then it is a worthy dwelling for King Reason, who will guide and direct it, and remain with it as long as the harmony is undisturbed. As soon, however, as this is impaired, he departs from it. A fool may imagine that Reason requires food, drink, and scents, because he sees himself preserved as long as these are forthcoming, but would perish if deprived of them. This is not the case. The Divine Influence is beneficent, and desirous of doing good to all. Wherever something is arranged and prepared to receive His guidance, He does not refuse it, nor withhold it, nor hesitate to shed light, wisdom, and inspiration on it. If, however, the order is disturbed, it cannot receive this light, which is, then, lost. The Divine Influence is above change or damage. All that is contained in the **order of sacrificial service**, its proceedings, offerings, burning of incense, singing, eating, drinking, is to be done in the utmost purity and holiness. It is called: Service of the Lord, the bread of thy God, and similar terms which relate to his pleasure in the beautiful harmony prevailing among the people and priesthood. He, so to say, accepts their hospitality and dwells among them in order to show them honour. He, however, is most Holy, and far too exalted to find pleasure in their meat and drink. It is for their own benefit, as is also the proper working order of the digestion in the stomach and liver. The nobler ingredients of the food go to strengthen the heart; the best of all, the spirit. Not only are heart, mind, and brain regenerated by means of this food, but also the digestive organs and all other organs through the strengthening matter which reaches them through the arteries, nerves and sinews. Altogether, this is so arranged and prepared, as to become fit to receive the guidance of the reasoning soul, which is an independent substance, and nearly approaches the angelic, of which it is stated: Its dwelling is not with flesh. It inhabits the body as ruler and guide, not in the sense of space, nor does it partake of this food, because it is exalted above it. The Divine Influence only dwells in a soul which is susceptible to intellect, whilst the soul only associates with the warm vital breath. The latter must needs have a mainspring to which it is attached, as is the flame to the top of the wick. The heart is compared to the wick, and is fed by the flow of blood. Blood is produced by the digestive organs, and therefore requires the stomach, the liver, and lower organs. The heart, in the same way, requires the lungs, throat, nose, the diaphragm, and the muscles which move the muscles of the chest for breathing, as well as to keep in balance the temperature of the heart between the air which enters, and that which is expelled. It further requires for the removal of the food, refuse expelling forces, viz. the excretory and urinary organs. In this way the body is formed from all the component parts mentioned. It also requires organs of motion from place to place, in order to procure its wants, to avoid that which is harmful, and to attract and to repel. It requires hands and feet, advisers who distinguish, warning against what is to be feared, and advising what is to be hoped for; who keep account of what has taken place, and record what has passed, in order to recommend care or hope for future events. It requires the internal and external senses, the seat of which is in the head, and which are assisted by the functions of the heart. The whole body is thus harmoniously arranged, but under the control of the heart, which forms the primary home of the soul. Its localization in the brain is of secondary importance, the heart remaining its regulator. In exactly the same way is the living, godly people arranged, as Yehoshua said: Hereby shall ye know that the living God is among you. The fire was kindled by the will of God, when the people found favour in His sight, being a sign that He accepted their hospitality and their offerings. For the fire is the finest and noblest element beneath the sphere of the moon. Its seat is the fat and vapour of sacrifices, the smoke of the incense and oil, as it is the nature of fire to cling to fat and oil. So also does natural heat cling to the finest fatty globules of the blood. God commanded the construction of the altar burnt offerings, the Altar of Incense, and the candlestick; their holocausts, incense, and the lamp oil. As regards the altar of burnt offerings, it was destined to bear the visible fire, whilst the Golden Altar was reserved for the invisible and finer fire. The candlestick was to bear the light of wisdom and inspiration; the table that of abundance and material provisions. The sages say: He who wishes to be wise must turn to the south; he who wishes to be rich must turn to the north. All these implements stood in the service of the Holy Ark and the Cherubim which occupied the place of the heart, and the lungs above it. The vessels, such as the laver and its foot, tongs, firepans, dishes, spoons, bowls, pots, and forks, etc., were all required. A place was wanted to house them, viz. the Tabernacle, tent and cover, and the court of the Tabernacle with its appurtenances, as an enclosure for the whole. As bearers of the entire household God appointed the Levites, because they were nearest to Him, especially after the affair of the golden calf, as it is said: And all the sons of Levi gathered themselves together unto Him. From among them He chose Elazar, the finest and noblest of them, as it is said: And to the office of Elazar the son of Aaron the priest pertaineth the oil for the light, and the sweet incense, and the daily meat offering, and the anointing oil - things to which the finer fire clings. The light of wisdom, however, and inspiration was attached to the Urim and Tummim, as well as to the most select section of Levites, viz. the family of Kohath, who carried the appurtenances of the internal service: the Ark, Table, Candlestick, Altars, and the Holy Vessels with which they served. With regard to them it is said: Because the service of the sanctuary belonged unto them, they should bear upon their shoulders - just as the internal organs of the body are without bones which help to carry them, but are, themselves, borne by the innate powers in conjunction with all that belongs to them. Another branch of the children of Gershon bore the more delicate external appurtenances, viz. the carpets of the Tabernacle, the Tent and its cover, and the covering of badger's skin that was above it. The lower section of the B'ne Merari bore the grosser utensils, viz. its hooks, boards, bars, pillars, and sockets. The last two sections were aided in carrying their burden by having chariots, as it is said: Two wagons for the Gershoni and four wagons for Merari according to their service. All this was systematically arranged by God. I do not, by any means, assert that the service was instituted in the order expounded by me, since it entailed something more secret and higher, and was based on a divine law. He who accepts this completely without scrutiny or argument, is better off than he who investigates and analyses. He, however, who steps down from the highest grade to scrutiny, does well to turn his face to the latent wisdom, instead of leading it to evil opinions and doubts which lead to corruption.

27. Al Khazari: Rebbi, thy symbolization was excellent, but the head and its senses, as well as the anointing oil were left unconsidered.

28. The Rebbi: Quite so. The root of all knowledge was deposited in the Ark which took the place of the heart, viz. the Ten Commandments, and its branch is the Torah on its side, as it is said: Put it in the side of the ark of the covenant of the Lord your God. From there went forth a twofold knowledge, firstly, the scriptural knowledge, whose bearers were the priests; secondly, the prophetic knowledge which was in the hands of the prophets. Both classes were, so to speak, the people's watchful advisers, who compiled the chronicles. They, therefore, represent the head of the people.

29. Al Khazari: So, you are to-day a body without either head or heart.

30. The Rebbi: Thou sayest rightly, but we are not even a body, only scattered limbs, like the dry bones which Ezekiel saw in his vision. These bones, however, O king of the Khazars, which have retained a trace of vital power, having once been the seat of a heart, brain, breath, soul, and intellect, are better than certain bodies formed of marble and plaster, endowed with heads, eyes, ears, and all limbs, in which never dwelt the spirit of life, nor ever can dwell in them, since they are but imitations of man, not man in reality.

31. Al Khazari: It is as thou sayest.

32. The Rebbi: The dead nations which desire to be held equal to the 'living' people can obtain nothing more than an external resemblance. They built houses for God, but no trace of Him was visible therein. They turned hermits and ascetics in order to secure inspiration, but it came not. They, then, deteriorated, became disobedient, and wicked; yet no fire fell down from heaven upon them, nor rapid pestilence, as a manifest punishment from God for their disobedience. Their heart, I mean the house in which they used to meet, was destroyed, but otherwise their status was not affected. This could only take place in accordance with the largeness or smallness of their number, with their strength or weakness, disunion or unity, following upon natural or accidental causes. We, however, since our heart, I mean the Holy House, was destroyed, were lost with it. If it be restored, we, too, will be restored, be we few or many, or in whichever way this may happen. For our master is the living God, our King, who keeps us in this our present condition in dispersion and exile.

33. Al Khazari: Certainly. A similar dispersion is not imaginable in any other people, unless it became absorbed by another, especially after so long a period. Many nations which arose after you have perished without leaving a memory, as Edom, Moab, Ammon, Aran, the Philistines, Chaldaeans, Medians, Persians, and Javan, the Brahmans, Sabaeans, and many others.

34. The Rebbi: Do not believe that I, though agreeing with thee, admit that we are dead. We still hold connexion with that Divine Influence through the laws which He has placed as a link between us and Him. There is circumcision, of which it is said: My covenant shall be in your flesh for an everlasting covenant. There is further the Sabbath, It is a sign between me and you throughout your generations. Besides this there is the covenant of the Fathers, and the covenant of the law, first granted on Horeb, and then in the plains of Moab in connexion with the promises and warnings laid down in the section: When thou shalt beget children and grandchildren. Compare further the antithesis: If any of thine be driven out unto the utmost parts of heaven; Thou shalt return unto the Lord thy God, finally, the song: Give ear; and other places. We are not like dead, but rather like a sick and attenuated person who has been given up by the physicians, and yet hopes for a miracle or an extraordinary recovery, as it is said: 'Can these bones live. Compare also the simile in the words: Behold my servant shall prosper; He has no form nor comeliness. Like one from whom men hid their faces; which means that he is, on account of his deformity and repulsive visage, compared to an unclean thing, which man only beholds with disgust, and turns away; Despised and rejected of men, A man of sorrows and acquainted with grief.

35. Al Khazari: How can this serve as a comparison for Israel, as it is said: Surely, he has borne our griefs. That which has befallen Israel has come to pass on account of its sins.

36. The Rebbi: Israel amidst the nations is like the heart amidst the organs of the body; it is at one and the same time the most-sick and the most-healthy of them.

37. Al Khazari: Make this a little clearer.

38. The Rebbi: The heart is exposed to all sorts of diseases, and frequently visited by them, such as sadness, anxiety, wrath, envy, enmity, love, hate, and fear. Its temperament changes continually, undulating between excess and deficiency, and moreover influenced by inferior nourishment, by movement, exertion, sleep, or wakefulness. They all affect the heart whilst the limbs rest.

39. Al Khazari: Now I understand how it can be the most-sick and most healthy of all organs simultaneously.

40. The Rebbi: Is it possible that it could suffer from swelling, or a cancer, or boils, a wound, weakness, and asthma, as is possible in other organs.

41. Al Khazari: Impossible. For the smallest trace of these would bring on death. Its extreme sensibility, caused by the purity of its blood, and its great intelligence causes it to feel the slightest symptom, and expels it as long as it is able to do so. The other organs lack this fine sensibility, and it is therefore possible that they can be affected by some strange matter which produces illness.

42. The Rebbi: Thus, its sensibility and feeling expose it to many ills, but they are at the same time the cause of their own expulsion at the very beginning, and before they have time to take root.

43. Al Khazari: Quite so.

44. The Rebbi: Our relation to the Divine Influence is the same as that of the soul to the heart. For this reason, it is said: You only have I known of all the families of the earth, therefore I will punish you for all your inquities. These are the illnesses. As regards its health, it is alluded to in the words of the sages: He forgives the sins of his people, causing the first of them to vanish first. He does not allow our sins to become overwhelming, or they would destroy us completely by their multitude. Thus, he says: For the iniquity of the Amorites is not yet full. He left them alone till the ailment of their sins had become fatal. Just as the heart is pure in substance and matter, and of even temperament, in order to be accessible to the intellectual soul, so also is Israel in its component parts. In the same way as the heart may be affected by disease of the other organs, viz. the lusts of the liver, stomach and genitals, caused through contact with malignant elements; thus, also is Israel exposed to ills originating in its inclinations towards the Gentiles. As it is said: They were mingled among the heathens and learned their works. Do not consider it strange if it is said in the same sense: Surely, he has borne our griefs and carried our sorrows. Now we are burdened by them, whilst the whole world enjoys rest and prosperity. The trials which meet us are meant to prove our faith, to cleanse us completely, and to remove all taint from us. If we are good, the Divine Influence is with us in this world. Thou knowest that the elements gradually evolved metals, plants, animals, man, finally the pure essence of man. The whole evolution took place for the sake of this essence, in order that the Divine Influence should inhabit it. That essence, however, came into existence for the sake of the highest essence, viz. the prophets and pious. A similar gradation can be observed in the prayer: Give thy fear, O Lord our God, over all Thy works. Then: Give glory to Thy people; finally: The pious shall see and rejoice, because they are the purest essence.

45. Al Khazari: Thy interesting comparison has completely riveted my attention. But I should expect to see more hermits and ascetics among you than among other people.

46. The Rebbi: I regret that thou hast forgotten those fundamental principles in which thou didst concur. Did we not agree that man cannot approach God except by means of deeds commanded by him. Dost, thou think that this can be gained by meekness, humility, etc., alone.

47. Al Khazari: Certainly, and rightly so. I think I read in your books as follows: What doth the Lord thy God require of thee, but to fear the Lord thy God. and What doth the Lord require of thee, and many similar passages.

48. The Rebbi: These are the rational laws,

being the basis and preamble of the divine law, preceding it in character and time, and being indispensable in the administration of every human society. Even a gang of robbers must have a kind of justice among them if their confederacy is to last. When Israel's disloyalty had come to such a pass that they disregarded rational and social principles, which are as absolutely necessary for a society as are the natural functions of eating, drinking, exercise, rest, sleeping, and waking for the individual, but held fast to the sacrificial worship and other divine laws, He was satisfied with even less. It was told to them: Haply you might observe those laws which rule the smallest and meanest community, such as refer to justice, good actions, and recognition of God's bounty. For the divine law cannot become complete till the social and rational laws are perfected. The rational law demands justice and recognition of God's bounty. What has he, who fails in this respect, to do with offerings, Sabbath, circumcision, etc., which reason neither demands, nor forbids. These are, however, the ordinations especially given to Israel as a corollary to the rational laws. Through this they received the advantage of the Divine Influence, without knowing how it came to pass that the 'Glory of God' descended upon them, and that 'the fire of God' consumed their offerings; how they heard the allocution of the Lord; and how their history developed. These are matters which reason would refuse to believe if they were not guaranteed by irrefutable evidence. In a similar sense it was said to them: 'What doth the Lord thy God require of thee. and add your burnt offerings, and similar verses. Can it be imagined that the Israelites observe the doing of justice and the love of mercy; but neglect circumcision, Sabbath, and the other laws, and felt happy withal.

49. Al Khazari: After what thou hast said I should not think so. In the opinion of philosophers, however, he becomes a pious man who does not mind in which way he approaches God, whether as a Jew or a Christian, or anything else he chooses. Now we have returned to reasoning, speculating and dialectics. According of this everyone might endeavour to belong to a creed dictated by his own speculating, a thing which would be absurd.

50. The Rebbi: The divine law imposes no asceticism on us. It rather desires that we should keep the equipoise, and grant every mental and physical faculty its due, as much as it can bear, without overburdening one faculty at the expense of another. If a person gives way to licentiousness, he blunts his mental faculty; he who is inclined to violence injures some other faculty. Prolonged fasting is no act of piety for a weak person who, having succeeded in checking his desires, is not greedy. For him feasting is a burden and self-denial. Neither is diminution of wealth an act of piety, if it is gained in a lawful way, and if its acquisition does not interfere with study and good works, especially for him who has a household and children. He may spend part of it in almsgiving, which would not be displeasing to God; but to increase it is better for himself. Our law, as a whole, is divided between fear, love, and joy, by each of which one can approach God. Thy contrition on a fast day does nothing the nearer to God than thy joy on the Sabbath and holy days, if it is the outcome of a devout heart. Just as prayers demand devotion, so also is a pious mind necessary to find pleasure in God's command and law; that thou shouldst be pleased with the law itself from love of the Lawgiver. Thou seest how much He has distinguished thee, as if thou hadst been His guest invited to His festive board. Thou thankest Him in mind and word, and if thy joy leads thee so far as to sing and dance, it becomes worship and a bond of union between thee and the Divine Influence. Our law did not consider these matters optional, but laid down decisive injunctions concerning them, since it is not in the power of mortal man to apportion to each faculty of the soul and body its right measure, nor to decide what amount of rest and exertion is good, or to determine how long the ground should be cultivated till it finds rest in the years of release and jubilee, or the amount of tithe to be given, etc. God commanded cessation of work on Sabbath and holy days, as well as in the culture of the soil, all this as a remembrance of the exodus from Egypt, and remembrance of the work of creation. These two things belong together, because they are the outcome of the absolute divine will, but not the result of accident or natural phenomena. It is said: For ask now of the days that are past- Did ever a people hear the voice of God-Or hath God assayed, etc. The observance of the Sabbath is itself an acknowledgment of His omnipotence, and at the same time an acknowledgment of the creation by the divine word. He who observes the Sabbath because the work of creation was finished on it acknowledges the creation itself. He who believes in the creation believes in the Creator. He, however, who does not believe in it falls a prey to doubts of God's eternity and to doubts of the existence of the world's Creator. The observance of the Sabbath is therefore nearer to God than monastic retirement and asceticism. Behold how the Divine Influence attached itself to Abraham, and then to all those who shared his excellence and the Holy Land. This Influence followed him everywhere, and guarded his posterity, preventing the detachment of any of them, it brought them to the most sheltered and best place, and caused them to multiply in a miraculous manner, and finally raised them to occupy a degree worthy of such excellence. He is, therefore, called: God of Abraham, God of the land. Dwelling between the Cherubim, dwelling in Zion, Abiding in Yerushalem, these places being compared to heaven, as it is said: Dwelling in heaven. His light shines in these places as in heaven, although through mediums which are fit to receive this light. He sheds it upon them, and this it is that is called love. It has been taught us, and we have been enjoined to believe in it, as well as to praise and thank Him in the prayer: "With eternal love Thou lovest us"; so that we should bear in mind that it originally came from Him, but not from us. To give an instance, we do not say that an animal created itself, but that God formed and fashioned it, having selected the proper matter for it. In the same manner it was He who initiated our delivery from Egypt to be His people and to acknowledge Him as king, as He said: I am the Lord your God who led you out of the land of Egypt to be unto you a God. He also says: O Israel, in whom I will be glorified.

51. Al Khazari: This sentence seems to go too far, and is overbold in expressing that the Creator is glorified through mortal man.

52. The Rebbi: Wouldst thou find this less strange in the creation of the sun.

53. Al Khazari: Certainly, on account of its great power. Next to God it is the cause of being. By its means night and day and the seasons of the year are determined; minerals, metals, plants, and animals were developed through its instrumentality. Its light produced sight and colours. Wherefore should not the action of such a thing be an object of glory among men.

54. The Rebbi: Are not the intellectual faculties much finer than the light that is seen? Or were not the inhabitants of the earth prior to the Israelites in blindness and error excepting those few whom I mentioned? Some people said that there was no Creator; that no part of the world was more worthy of being created than being creator, the universe being eternal. Others say that the spheres are eternal and creative. They consequently adore them. Others again assert that the fire is the essence of light and all the miraculous products of its power; it must, therefore, be worshipped. The soul also is fire. Others worship different things, viz. sun, moon, stars, and animal forms, which are in connexion with special phenomena. Other people adore their kings and sages. They all, however, agree that there is nothing in the world which is contrary to nature, nor is there any Providence. Even philosophers who, with their refined intuition and clear view, acknowledge a Prime Cause

| Kuzari | Second Essay |

different from earthly things and unparalleled, are inclined to think that this Prime Cause exercises no influence on the world, and certainly not on individuals, as he is too exalted to know them, much less to make them the basis of a new entity. The community was at last considered sufficiently pure for the light to dwell on it, to be worthy of seeing miracles which changed the course of nature, and to understand that the world had a King who watched and guarded it, who knew both great and small, rewarded the good and the wicked, and directed the hearts. All who came after these philosophers could not detach themselves from their principles, so that to-day the whole civilized world acknowledges that God is eternal, and that the world was created. They look upon the Israelites and all that befell them as a proof of this.

55. Al Khazari: This is glory indeed, and an extraordinary proof. It is justly written: To make Himself an everlasting name, so didst Thou get Thee a name as it is this day, and in praise, in name, and in honour.

56. The Rebbi: Didst thou not see how David introduces the praise of the Toroh, when he first speaks of the sun in the words: The heavens declare the glory of God. He describes how ubiquitous its light, how pure its body, how steady its path, and beautiful its countenance. This is followed by the words: The law of the Lord is perfect, etc., as if he wished to convey that one should not wonder at such a description. For the Torah is more pure, more resplendent, more widely known, more exalted, and more useful still. If there were no Israelites there would be no Torah. They did not derive their high position from Moshe, but Moshe received his for their sake. The divine love dwelt among the descendants of Abraham, Itzhak, and Yaakov. The choice of Moshe, however, was made in order that the good fortune might come to them through his instrumentality. We are not called the people of Moshe, but the people of God, as it is said: The people of the Lord. And the people of the God of Abraham. Proof of the Divine Influence is not found in well chosen words, in raising the eyebrows, closing the eyes during prayers, contrition, movement, and talk behind which there are no deeds; but a pure mind, illustrated by corresponding actions which, by their very nature, are difficult to perform, and are yet performed with the utmost zeal and love. It is to be found in one who, wherever he may, strives to reach the chosen place three times a year, and bearing with the greatest pleasure and joy all fatigues and expenses connected therewith. He pays the **first tithe**, and the **second tithe** and the **poor tithe**, and the expenses connected with his apparel for the

Temple. He renounces the harvest in the years of release and jubilee, incurs expense for a tabernacle, holy days, and abstention from work; gives the first fruits, the firstborn animals, priests' emoluments, the first of the shearing, and the first of the dough, apart from vows and free gifts, and fines connected with intentional and unintentional sins, and peace offerings. Further offerings due on account of private happenings, impurity, child-bed, issue, leprosy, and many other things. All this is regulated by divine command, without human speculation. It is not possible for man to determine the relative importance of each, and he need not fear any deterioration in them. It is as if He assessed Israel, and measured them as well as the harvests of Palestine as regards vegetable and animal life. He also considered the tribe of Levi, and ordained these assessments in the desert, because he knew that, as long as they were not infringed, Israel would retain its surplus, and the Levite would not be in want. It never could come to such a pass that a tribe or family would be reduced to poverty, because he ordained the return of the whole property in the year of jubilee in the same status as it was in the first year of the distribution of the land. The details of these regulations would fill volumes. He who studies them carefully will see that they are not of human origin. Praised be He who has contrived them: He hath not dealt so with any nation; they are judgments which they knew not. This arrangement lasted during the periods of both Temples for about 1,300 years, and had the people remained in the straight path, it would have been as the days of the heaven on earth.

57. Al Khazari: At present you are in great confusion concerning those heavy duties. What nation could observe such regulations.

58. The Rebbi: The community whose guardian and compensator is always in its midst-I mean God. Yehoshua said: You cannot serve the Lord, for He is an holy God. Notwithstanding this, his community was so zealously observing that, in the matter of the trespass of 'the devoted thing of Jericho,' not more than the one, Achan, was found disobedient among more than six hundred thousand. The punishment followed immediately, just as it did in the case of Miriam, who was afflicted with leprosy; also, in the cases of Uzzah, Nadab and Abihu, and the people of Beth-Shemesh, who were punished because they had looked into the ark of the Lord. It was one of the wonderful traits of God that His displeasure for minor transgressions was shown on the walls of houses and in the clothes, whilst for more grievous sins the bodies were more or less severely stricken. The priests were appointed to study this profound science and to discover to what extent these trials were God's punishment this often took them weeks to find out, as was the case with Miriam, or how much was simply constitutionally curable or incurable. This is an abstruse science to which God pointed in the words: Take heed in the plague of leprosy, that thou observe diligently and do according to all that the priests, the Levites, shall teach you.

59. Al Khazari: Hast thou a satisfactory argument on the matter.

60. The Rebbi: I told thee that there is no comparison to be made between our intelligence and the Divine Influence, and it is proper that we leave the cause of these important things unexamined. I take, however, the liberty of stating-though not with absolute certainty-that leprosy and issue are occasionally the consequence of contamination by corpses. A dead body represents the highest degree of malignancy, and a leprous limb is as if dead. It is the same with lost sperm, because it had been endowed with living power, capable of engendering a human being. Its loss, therefore, forms a contrast to the living and breathing, and on account of its ideal potentiality only affects noble minds and highly strung souls which incline towards the divine, prophetic, visionary, and towards genuine imagination. There are people who feel depressed as long as they have not purified themselves after such an accident. Experience has taught them that their touch deteriorates such fine things as pearls and wine. Most of us feel influenced by the vicinity of dead bodies and graves, and our spirits are depressed as long as we find ourselves in a house in which there is a corpse. Those of coarser mould remain untouched. We see the same in intellectual matters. He who seeks purity of thought in philosophic studies, or purity of soul in prayer, feels uncomfortable in the association with women and scoffers, or during the recitation of jocular or love songs.

61. Al Khazari: This explains to me why the physical birthright, viz. the sperm, contaminates, though being wholly spiritual, whilst other excreta do not do so, in spite of their repulsive aspect, odour, and quantity. Now I should still like to hear the explanation of the leprosy of the garment and the house.

62. The Rebbi: I mentioned that as one of the characteristics of the Shekhinah, that it occupies in Israel the same place as the spirit of life in the human body. It granted them a divine life, and allowed them to find lustre, beauty, and light in their souls, bodies, dispositions, and houses. When it was absent from them, their intelligence waned, their bodies deteriorated, and their beauty faded. The effect of the disappearance of the divine light became noticeable in every individual. One can easily see how the breath of a person is suddenly lost through fear and sorrow, whereby the body also suffers. On women and boys who go out at night one may sometimes see black and green marks, the result of their weak nerves. This is attributed to demons, but diseases of body and mind are often produced by the sight of people who have died or were killed.

63. Al Khazari: I perceive that your law comprises all sorts of profound and strange sciences, -not to be found in other codes.

64. The Rebbi: The members of the Synhedrion were bound not to let any science, real and fictitious, or conventional, escape their knowledge, magic and language included. How was it possible at all times to find seventy scholars unless learning was common among the people? If one elder died, another of the same stamp succeeded him. This could not be otherwise, as all branches of science were required for the practice of the law. Natural sciences was wanted for agriculture, in order to recognise 'mingled seed,' to be careful with the produce of the seventh year and of newly planted trees, to distinguish the various kinds of plants, that their nature might be preserved, and one species be not mixed up with another. It is difficult enough to know whether chondros is a kind of barley, or spelt, a kind of wheat, or brassica is a kind of cabbage; to study the powers of their roots and how far they spread in the ground; how much of it remains for the following year, and how much does not remain; how much space and time is to be left between each species. Further, the distinction of the various species of animals served various purposes, among which is to know which communicates poison and which not. With this is connected the knowledge of injuries which make an animal unlawful for food. This is even more profound than what Aristotle wrote on the subject, viz. how to know which injuries are fatal and thus to deter people from eating carrion. The small remnant of this knowledge which has remained makes us wonder. Add to this the acquaintance with the blemishes which disqualify priests from taking part in the Temple service, as well as of the blemishes which prohibit the offering up of certain animals as sacrifices. Then there is the knowledge of the various kinds of issue and of the period of purification. All this requires instruction. Man is not able to determine these matters by reflection alone, without divine assistance. The same is the case with the knowledge of the revolutions of the spheres, of which the yearly calendar is but one fruit. The excellence of the calculation of the calendar is famous, and it is well known what deep root it has taken among these people, few in number, yet excellently equipped with model institutions. Could it be otherwise? On account of the smallness, humbleness, and dispersion of the people it is hardly noticed among the other nations, yet those relics of the Divine made it into one firmly established organization. The calendar, based on the rules of the revolution of the moon, as handed down by the House of David, is truly wonderful. Though hundreds of years have passed, no mistake has been found in it, whilst the observations of Greek and other astronomers are not faultless. They were obliged to insert corrections and supplements every century, whilst our calendar is always free from error, as it rests on prophetic tradition. Had there been the smallest flaw in a fundamental rule this would to-day have assumed serious proportions, on account of the time difference between the conjunction of the moon and the moment when she becomes visible. In the same manner our sages were, without doubt, acquainted with the movements of the sun and astronomy in general. Music was the pride of a nation which distributed their songs in such a way that they fell to the lot of the aristocracy of the people, viz. the Levites, who made practical use of them in the holy house and in the holy season. For their maintenance they were satisfied with the tithes, as they had no occupation but music. As an art it is highly esteemed among mankind, as long as it is not abused and degraded, and as long as the people preserves its original nobleness and purity. David and Samuel were its great masters. Dost, thou think that they understood it well or not.

65. Al Khazari: There can be no doubt that their art was most perfect, and touched the souls, as people say that it changes the humour of a man's soul to a different one. It is impossible that it should now reach the same high level. It has deteriorated, and servants and half-crazy people are its patrons. Truly, Rebbi, it sank from its greatness, as you have sunk in spite of your former greatness.

66. The Rebbi: What is thy opinion of Shlomo's accomplishments? Did he not, with the assistance of divine, intellectual, and natural power, converse on all sciences? The inhabitants of the earth travelled to him, in order to carry forth his learning, even as far as India. Now the roots and principles of all sciences were handed down from us first to the Chaldaeans, then to the Persians and Medians, then to Greece, and finally to the Romans. On account of the length of this period, and the many disturbing circumstances, it was forgotten that they had originated with the Hebrews, and so they were ascribed to the Greeks and Romans. To Hebrew, however, belongs the first place, both as regards the nature of the languages, and as to fullness of meanings.

67. Al-Khazari: Is Hebrew superior to other languages, do we not see distinctly that the latter are more finished and comprehensive.

68. The Rebbi: It shared the fate of its bearers, degenerating and dwindling with them. Considered historically and logically, its original form is the noblest. According to tradition it is the language in which God spoke to Adam and Eve, and in which the latter conversed. It is proved by the derivation of Adam from adamah, ishshah from ish; hayyah from hayy; Cain from qanithi; Sheth from shath, and Noah from yenah, menu. This is supported by the evidence of the Torah. The whole is traced back to Eber, Noah and Adam. It is the language of Eber after whom it was called Hebrew, because after the confusion of tongues it was he who retained it. Abraham was an Aramaean of Ur Kasdim, because the language of the Chaldaeans was Aramaic. He employed Hebrew as an especially holy language and Aramaic for everyday use. For this reason, Ishmael brought it to the Arabic speaking nations, and the consequence was that Aramaic, Arabic and Hebrew are similar to each other in their vocabulary, grammatical rules, and formations. The superiority of Hebrew is manifest from the logical point of view if we consider the people who employed it for discourses, particularly at the time when prophecy was rife among them, also for preaching, songs and psalmody. It is conceivable that their rulers such as for instance, Moshe, Yehoshua, David, and Shlomo lacked the words to express what they wished, as it is the case with us to-day, because it is lost to us? Dost thou not see how the Torah, when describing the Tabernacle, Ephod and breastplate and other objects, always finds the most suitable word for all these strange matters? How beautifully is this description composed? It is just the same with the names of people, species of birds and stones, the diction of David's Psalms, the lamentations of Job, and his dispute with his friends, the addresses of Isaiah, etc.

69. Al-Khazari: Thou wilt only succeed in placing it on a par with other languages thus. But where is its pre-eminence? Other languages surpass it in songs metrically constructed and arranged for tunes.

70. The Rebbi: It is obvious that a tune is independent of the metre, or of the lesser or greater number of syllables. The verse hōdū la'donai ki tob can, therefore, be sung to the same tune as - leose niflaeth gedoloth lebaddo. This is the rule in sentences in which the tune must follow the grammatical construction. Rhymed poems, however, which are recited,

and in which a good metre is noticeable, are neglected for something higher and more useful.

71. Al-Khazari: And what may that be.

72. The Rebbi: The faculty of speech is to transmit the idea of the speaker into the soul of the hearer. Such intention, however, can only be carried out to perfection by means of oral communication. This is better than writing. The proverb is: From the mouths of scholars, but not from the mouth of books. Verbal communication finds various aids either in pausing or continuing to speak, according to the requirements of the sentence, by raising or lowering the voice, in expressing astonishment, question, narrative, desire, fear or submission by means of gestures, without which speech by itself would remain inadequate. Occasionally the speaker even has recourse to movements of eyes, eyebrows, or the whole head and hands, in order to express anger, pleasure, humility or haughtiness to the degree desired. In the remnant of our language which was created and instituted by God, are implanted subtle elements calculated to promote understanding, and to take the place of the above aids to speech. These are the accents with which the holy text is read. They denote pause and continuation, they separate question from answer, the beginning from the continuation of the speech, haste from hesitation, command from request, on which subject books might be written. He who intends to do this must omit poetry, because it can only be recited in one way. For it mostly connects when it should stop and stops where it should go on. One cannot avoid this except with great trouble.

73. Al-Khazari: It is but proper that mere beauty of sound should yield to lucidity of speech. Harmony pleases the ear, but exactness makes the meaning clear. I see, however, that you Jews long for a prosody, in imitation of other peoples, in order to force the Hebrew language into their metres.

74. The Rebbi: This is because we remained and are froward. Instead of being satisfied with the superiority mentioned above, we corrupted the structure of our language, which is built on harmony, and created discord.

75. Al-Khazari: How so.

76. The Rebbi: Didst thou not see that a hundred persons read the Torah as one person, stopping in one moment, and continuing simultaneously.

77. Al-Khazari: I have, indeed, observed this, and never saw the like of it either among

Persians or Arabs. It is impossible in the recitation of a poem. Now I should like to know how the Hebrew language obtained that advantage, and how the metre interferes with it.

78. The Rebbi: The reason is that you can put together two vowelless consonants, but not three vowels, except in rare cases This not only gives the speech a rest, but enables it to obtain that advantage, viz. consonance and fluency in reading. This makes learning by heart and the grasping of the meaning easy. The first thing which destroys metrical reading is the relation of those two consonants. Correct accentuation becomes impossible, so that **okhlah** [food] is read like **okhelah** [she is eating]; **omro** [his word] and **ameru** [they have spoken] have metrically the same value as **omer** [speaking] and **omer** [word]. Thus, also the time difference between shabti, which is past tense, and we shabti, which is future, lost. We might find a way out of this difficulty if we followed the ways of the Piyyut which does not interfere with the language, and merely employs the rhyme. But in matters of poetry, the same befell us which befell our forefathers, concerning whom it is written: They mingled among the gentiles and learned their works.

79. Al-Khazari: I should like to ask whether thou knowest the reason why Jews move to and fro when reading the Torah.

80. The Rebbi: It is said that it is done in order to arouse natural heat. My personal belief is that it stands in connexion with the subject under discussion. As it often happened that many persons read at the same time, it was possible that ten or more read from one volume. This is the reason why our books are so large. Each of them was obliged to bend down in his turn in order to read a passage, and to turn back again. This resulted in a continual bending and sitting up, the book lying on the ground. This was one reason. Then it became a habit through constant seeing, observing and imitating, which is in man's nature. Other people read each out of his own book, either bringing it near to his eyes, or, if he pleased, bending down to it without inconveniencing his neighbour. There was, therefore, no necessity of bending and sitting up. We will now discuss the importance of the accents, the orthographic value of the seven principal vowel signs, the grammatical accuracy resulting from them as well as from the distinction between Qameṣ, Pataḥ, Ṣere and Segol. They influence the meaning of grammatical forms and assist in distinguishing between past and future tenses, שַׂמְתִּי and וְשַׂמְתִּי and וָאֲבָרְכֵהוּ and וְאֲבָרְכֵהוּ. Or between a verb and an adjective, חָבַם and חָכָם; between the interrogative He and the article, as in הַעוֹלָה הִיא לְמַעְלָה, and other cases. The euphony and structure of speech is increased by the sequence of two vowelless consonants, which enables a whole congregation to read Hebrew simultaneously without mistakes. Other rules apply to the musical accents. For the vowel sounds are divided in Hebrew into three classes, viz. U-sound, A-sound, and I-sound; or in another division: great U-sound, or Qameṣ, medium U-sound, or Ḥolem; little U-sound, or Shureq; great A-sound, or Pataḥ; little A-sound or Segol; great I-sound or Sere; little I-sound, or Ḥireq. Shewa is sounded with all these vowels under certain conditions. It is vowel absolute, because any addition would require a vowelless consonant to follow. Qameṣ is followed by a long-closed syllable, but not by dagesh in the first form Dagesh can only follow, if demanded by the exigencies of the second or third forms, the syllable being long, by one of the vowel letters alef or he, as in ברא and קנה. A syllable of this kind can also end in a vowelless consonant, as in קאם. Ḥolem also can be followed by a vowel letter which is waw or alef as in לא and לו, or a syllable of this kind can be closed by a consonant as שׁור and שְׂמֹאל. The vowel letters after Ṣere are alef or yod as in יוצא and יוצאי. He, however, only in the second form, but not in the first. Shureq is free for all three forms. It can be followed by a vowel letter, or dagesh, or vowelless consonant. Its long vowel is expressed by waw only as, לו, ללון and לָקַח. Ḥireq follows the rule of Shureq as in לין, לי and לבי. Pataḥ, and Segol are not followed by a vowel letter in the first form, but are lengthened by the second form, either for the sake of emphasis, or on account of the accent, or in the pause at the end of a sentence. The rules of the first form are obtained by considering the formation of each word separately, without any relation to the construction of the sentence with its variety of combination and separation, and long and short words. Then are obtained the seven principal vowels in their original, unchanged form and the simple Shewa without qa'ya. The second form deals with euphony in the construction of sentences. Occasionally elements of the first form are altered to please the second. The third form concerns the accents, and sometimes reacts on both preceding ones. In the first form three consecutive vowels without an intervening consonant or dagesh are possible, but three, or more, short vowels may follow each other as in Arabic. This, however, is impossible in the second form. As soon as three vowels follow each other in the first form, the second one lengthens one of them to the quantity of a long vowel as in לשְׁבֵנִי, מִשְׁבָּנִי, רצפת. For Hebrew does not allow three consecutive vowels, except when a consonant is either repeated as in שררך, or in the case of gutturals as in נהרי and נחלי, the reader being at liberty to read the first syllable long or short. In the same way the first form allows the sequence of two long closed syllables. The second form, however, to prevent clumsiness of speech, shortens one long syllable as in שמתי and ושמתי. It is obvious that the pronunciation of פעל and similar forms is contrary to its vocalisation, the second syllable being lengthened in spite of the Pataḥ, whilst the first is read short in spite of the Qameṣ. The heightening of the second syllable is due to the tone, but not to make it slightly longer. Words as אמר-לי and עשה-לי remain therefore in the first form, because the smaller word has the tone. We also find פָּעָל with two Qameṣ though in the past tense. The cause of this is to be found in the athnaḥ or sof pasuq, and we say that this is possible in the second form on account of the pause. We follow this up till we find even פָּעָל with two Qameṣ and zaqef. The reason of this we find in a virtual pause, the word being entitled to athnaḥ or sof pasuq, but other cogent reasons made athnaḥ and sof pasuq in this case impossible. On the other hand we find these two accents with two pataḥs, however strange this may be, e.g. וַיֹּאמַר, וַיֵּלֶךְ, וַתִּשְׁבַּרְנָה, וְזָקַנְתִּי. The reason of pataḥ in ויאמר is found in examining its meaning, as it cannot stand in pause, and is necessarily connected with the following complement of the sentence There are only a few exceptions as כַּאֲשֶׁר אָמָר, because the verb completes the sentence logically, and can take Qameṣ because of the pause. As regards, however, וילך and ותשברנה, they should originally be וַיֵּלֶךְ and

ותשבֵּרנה; but the transformation of the I-sound with great Paṭaḥ, without any intermediate element, was too awkward, and therefore Paṭaḥ stepped in. The form זקנתי belongs probably to the same class, because the root is זָקֵן, the Ṣere being changed into Paṭaḥ at the end of a sentence. We marvel why the פֶּעֶל forms have the accent on the first syllable which is read long, although it has Segol. We must, however, consider that, if the first syllable remained short, Hebrew phonology would require the second syllable to be read long and with accent, and a slight quiescent would creep in between the second and third radicals. This would be inelegant, which is not the case in the first syllable, which must have this quiescent and has also room for it. This lengthening of the penultima corresponds to כֶּן עֶל, but not to פֶּן עֶל. For when the word has athnaḥ, or sof pasuq, it is פָּעֶל corresponding to פָּאן עֶל. This shows the necessity of lengthening the vowel in שַמתי and שָמתי. We consider forms like שער and נער likewise strange, because the Paṭaḥ of the first syllable is read long. We soon discover, however, that they are פֶּעֶל forms with Paṭaḥ on account of the guttural. For this reason, they undergo no change in the status constructus, as do נהר and קהל, which are formed like דָבָר. Then we find אעשה ,יעשה, אבנה and אקנה with Sēgōl and vowel letters. If we consider the first instance, we find it to be a form אפעל, יפעל, the second radical not being long, but always forming a closed syllable with Paṭaḥ. We are now to read אעֱשֶׂה instead of Paṭaḥ, because no A-sound can precede a silent he, unless it be Qameṣ. Qameṣ is long, whilst the second radical of a verb can never have a long vowel, except when read with a vowel, or when followed by Alef as in אֵצֵא. It is for this reason that אעשה is read with Segol which is the shortest vowel imaginable, but interchanges with Ṣere when the second form requires to replace the one by the other at the ends of sentences. There is almost no necessity for the he of אעשה except in the pause or with the accent, and is eased by dagesh as in אעשה-לך and אבנה-לי, in which cases the he has no function. This is not the case [with א] in אצא, אבא. In בא-לי, there is no dagesh, the א being preceded by Ṣere and being a radical. He, however, is considered to be so weak that it is both graphically and phonetically omitted in ויבן, ויקן and ויעש. How could it, then, close a syllable vocalized by Ṣere? It was, therefore, left to Segol, the slightest vowel, at all events, in the first form. The second form changed it into Sere, when standing in pause. It appears likewise strange that מקנה, מעשה, מראה and similar forms have Ṣere in the construct state, but Segol in the absolute. We should think the reverse to be correct. But if we consider that the third radical, viz. a silent He is treated as altogether absent, and those nouns have the forms of מקן, מעש, מרא, nothing but Segol will serve till some circumstances bring it out with a long vowel as in מְרָאֵיהֶן, מַעֲשֶׂה, מַרְאֶה and מַעֲשֵׂיהֶן. Segol becomes Ṣere to take the place of small Pataḥ in מַרְאֶם and מַעֲשֶׂם. Words of the first form can be altered by the second as to the vowels, but not as to the pronunciation. The word בֵּן has Ṣere in the absolute state, Segol in the construct. Occasionally the latter is lengthened by the tone as in בֶּן-יָאִיר, with the Segol of the first form In other cases the tone precipitates it, although it has Ṣere according to the first form, as in בֶּן אַחֵר. In segolate forms with the accent on the last syllable Ṣere is no longer perplexing. The author of this profound science held secrets which are unknown to us. We may have discovered some by means of which he intended to stimulate our investigation as we have said above, with regard to הָעוֹלָה הִיא לְמַעְלָה. Or we might find out the rules of distinguishing between past and future, infinitive and participle of the passive voice, נֶאֱסָף אֶל עַמִּי, with Qameṣ, and נֶאֱשַׁר נֶאֱסַף with Pataḥ. The masoretic text vocalizes three times וַיִּשְׁקָט, with Qameṣ, although syntactically speaking the words stand only virtually in pause. There are many instances that the Segol after Zarqa has the force of Athnaḥ, or sof pasuq, or Zakef, causing an alteration of the first form. If I wished to enlarge the subject, the book would become too lengthy. I only desired to give thee a taste of this profound study, which is not built on haphazard, but on fixed rules.

81. Al Khazari: This is sufficient to enlighten me on the wonderful character of the Hebrew language. Now I desire the description of a servant of God according to your conception. Afterwards I will ask thee for thy arguments against the Karaites. Then I should like to hear the principal articles of faith and religious axioms. Finally, I wish to know which branches of ancient study have been preserved among you.

Kuzari　　　　　　　　　　　Second Essay

Third Essay

1. The Rebbi: According to our view a servant of God is not one who detaches himself from the world, lest he be a burden to it, and it to him; or hates life, which is one of God's bounties granted to him, as it is written: The number of thy days I will fulfill; Thou shalt live long. On the contrary, he loves the world and a long life, because it affords him opportunities of deserving the world to come. The more-good he does the greater is his claim to the next world. He even reaches the degree of Enoch, concerning whom it is said: And Enoch walked with God; or the degree of Eliyahu, freed from worldly matters, and to be admitted to the realm of angels. In this case he feels no loneliness in solitude and seclusion, since they form his associates. He is rather ill at ease in a crowd, because he misses the divine presence which enables him to dispense with eating and drinking. Such persons might perhaps be happier in complete solitude; they might even welcome death, because it leads to the step beyond which there is none higher. Philosophers and scholars also love solitude to refine their thoughts, and to reap the fruits of truth from their researches, in order that all remaining doubts be dispelled by truth. They only desire the society of disciples who stimulate their research and retentiveness, just as he who is bent upon making money would only surround himself with persons with whom he could do lucrative business. Such a degree is that of Socrates and those who are like him. There is no one nowadays who feels tempted to strive for such a degree, but when the Divine Presence was still in the Holy Land among the people capable of prophecy, some few persons lived an ascetic life in deserts and associated with people of the same frame of mind. They did not seclude themselves completely, but they endeavoured to find support in the knowledge of the Law and in holy and pure actions which brought them near to that high rank. These were the disciples of prophets. He, however, who in our time, place, and people, 'whilst no open vision exists, the desire for study being small, and persons with a natural talent for it absent, would like to retire into ascetic solitude, only courts distress and sickness for soul and body. The misery of sickness is visibly upon him, but one might regard it as the consequence of humility and contrition. He considers himself in prison as it were, and despairs of life from disgust of his prison and pain, but not because he enjoys his seclusion. How could it be otherwise? He has no intercourse with the divine light, and cannot associate himself with it as the prophets. He lacks the necessary learning to be absorbed in it and to enjoy it, as the philosophers did, all the rest of his life. Suppose he is God-fearing, righteous, desires to meet his God in solitude, standing, humbly and contritely, reciting as many prayers and supplications as he possibly can remember, all this affords him satisfaction for a few days as long as it is new. Words frequently repeated by the tongue lose their influence on the soul, and he cannot give to the latter humbleness or submission. Thus, he remains night and day, whilst his soul urges him to employ its innate powers in seeing, hearing, speaking, occupation, eating, cohabitation, gain, managing his house, helping the poor, upholding the law with money in case of need. Must he not regret those things to which he has tied his soul, a regret which tends to remove him from the Divine Influence, which he desired to approach.

2. Al Khazari: Give me a description of the doings of one of your pious men at the present time.

3. The Rebbi: A pious man is, so to speak, the guardian of his country, who gives to its inhabitant's provisions and all they need. He is so just that he wrongs no one, nor does he grant anyone more than his due. Then, when he requires them, he finds them obedient to his call. He orders, they execute; he forbids, they abstain.

4. Al Khazari: I asked thee concerning a pious man, not a prince.

5. The Rebbi: The pious man is nothing but a prince who is obeyed by his senses, and by his mental as well as his physical faculties, which he governs corporeally, as it is written: He that ruleth his spirit is better than he that taketh a city. He is fit to rule, because if he were the prince of a country he would be as just as he is to his body and soul. He subdues his passions, keeping them in bonds, but giving them their share in order to satisfy them as regards food, drink, cleanliness, etc. He further subdues the desire for power, but allows them as much expansion as avails them for the discussion of scientific or mundane views, as well as to warn the evil-minded. He allows the senses their share according as he requires them for the use of hands, feet, and tongue, as necessity or desire arise. The same is the case with hearing, seeing, and the kindred sensations which succeed them; imagination, conception, thought, memory, and will power, which commands all these; but is, in its turn, subservient to the will of intellect. He does not allow any of these limbs or faculties to go beyond their special task, or encroach upon another. If he, then, has satisfied each of them, giving to the vital organs the necessary amount of rest and sleep, and to the physical ones waking, movements, and worldly occupation, he calls upon his community as a respected prince calls his disciplined army, to assist him in reaching the higher or divine degree which is to be found above the degree of the intellect. He arranges his community in the same manner as Moshe arranged his people round Mount Sinai. He orders his will power to receive every command issued by him obediently, and to carry it out forthwith. He makes faculties and limbs do his bidding without contradiction, forbids them evil inclinations of mind and fancy, forbids them to listen to, or believe in them, until he has taken counsel with the intellect. If he permits, they can obey him, but not otherwise. In this way his will power receives its orders from him, carrying them out accordingly. He directs the organs of thought and imagination, relieving them of all worldly ideas mentioned above, charges his imagination to produce, with the assistance of memory, the most splendid pictures possible, in order to resemble the divine things sought after. Such pictures are the scenes of Sinai, Abraham and Itzhak on mountain of Moriah, the Tabernacle of Moshe, the Temple service, the presence of God in the Temple, and the like. He, then, orders his memory to retain all these, and not to forget them; he warns his fancy and its sinful prompters not to confuse the truth or to trouble it by doubts; he warns his irascibility and greed not to influence or lead astray, nor to take hold of his will, nor subdue it to wrath and lust. As soon as harmony is restored, his will power stimulates all his organs to obey it with alertness, pleasure, and joy. They stand without fatigue when occasion demands, they bow down when he bids them to do so, and sit at the proper moment. The eyes look as a servant looks at his master, the hands drop their play and do not meet, the feet stand straight, and all limbs are as frightened and anxious to obey their master, paying no heed to pain or injury. The tongue agrees with the thought, and does not overstep its bounds, does not speak in prayer in a mere mechanical way as the starling and the parrot, but every word is uttered thoughtfully and attentively. This moment forms the heart and fruit of his time, whilst the other hours represent the way which leads to it. He looks forward to its approach, because while it lasts, he resembles the spiritual beings, and is removed from merely animal existence. Those three times of daily prayer are the fruit of his day and night, and the Sabbath is the fruit of the week, because it has been appointed to establish the connexion with the Divine Spirit and to serve God in joy, not in sadness, as has been explained before. All this stands in the same relation to the soul as food to the human body. Prayer is for his soul what nourishment is for his body. The blessing of one prayer lasts till the time of the next, just as the strength derived from the morning meal lasts till supper. The further his soul is removed from the time of prayer, the more it is darkened by coming in contact with worldly matters. The more so, as necessity brings it into the company of youths, women, or wicked people; when one hears unbecoming and soul-darkening words and songs which exercise an attraction for his soul which he is unable to master. During prayer he purges his soul from all that passed over it, and prepares it for the future. According to this arrangement there elapses not a single week in which both his soul and body do not receive preparation. Darkening elements having increased during the week, they cannot be cleansed except by consecrating one day to service and to physical rest. The body repairs on the Sabbath the waste suffered during the six days, and prepares itself for the work to come, whilst the soul remembers its own loss through the body's companionship. He cures himself, so to speak, from a past illness, and provides himself with a remedy to ward off any future sickness. This is almost the same as Job did with his children every week, as it is written: It may be that my sons have sinned. He, then, provides himself with a monthly cure, which is - the season of atonement for all that happened during this period, viz. the duration of the month, and the daily events, as it is written: Thou knowest not what a day may bring forth. He further attends the Three Festivals and the great Fast Day, on which some of his sins are atoned for, and on which he endeavours to make up for what he may have missed on the days of those weekly and monthly circles. His soul frees itself from the whisperings of imagination, wrath, and lust, and neither in thought or deed gives them any attention. Although his soul is unable to atone for sinful thoughts-the result of songs, tales, etc., heard in youth, and which cling to memory-it cleanses itself from real sins, confesses repentance for the former, and undertakes to allow them no more to escape his tongue, much less to put them into practice, as it is written: I am purposed that my mouth shall not transgress. The fast of this day is such as brings one near to the angels, because it is spent in humility and contrition, standing, kneeling, praising and singing. All his physical faculties are denied their natural requirements, being entirely abandoned to religious service, as if the animal element had disappeared. The fast of a pious man is such that eye, ear, and tongue share in it, that he regards nothing except that which brings him near to God. This also refers to his innermost faculties, such as mind and imagination. To this he adds pious works.

6. Al Khazari: Dost thou refer to deeds generally known.

7. The Rebbi: The social and rational laws are those generally known. The divine ones, however, which were added in order that they should exist in the people of the **Living God** who guides them, were not known until they were explained in detail by Him. Even those social and rational laws are not quite known, and though one might know the gist of them, their scope remains unknown. We know that the giving of comfort and the feeling of gratitude are as incumbent on us as is chastening of the soul by means of fasting and meekness; we also know that deceit, immoderate intercourse with women, and cohabitation with relatives are abominable; that honouring parents is a duty, etc. The limitation of all these things to the amount of general usefulness is God's. Human reason is out of place in matters of divine action, on account of its incapacity to grasp them. Reason must rather obey, just as a sick person must obey the physician in applying his medicines and advice. Consider how little circumcision has to do with philosophy, and how small is its social influence. Yet Abraham, in spite of the hardship the very nature of this command must have seemed at his age, subjected his person and children to it, and it became the sign of the covenant, of the attachment of the Divine Influence to him, as it is written: And I will establish My covenant between me and thee and thy seed after them in their generations, for an everlasting covenant, to be a God unto thee….

8. Al Khazari: You accepted this command in a proper manner indeed, and you perform it publicly with the greatest zeal and readiness, praising it and expressing its root and origin in the formula of blessing. Other nations may desire to imitate you, but they only have the pain without the joy which can only be felt by him who remembers the cause for which he bears the pain.

9. The Rebbi: Even in other instances of imitation no people can equal us at all. Look at the others who appointed a day of rest in the place of Sabbath. Could they contrive anything which resembles it more than statues resemble living human bodies.

10. Al Khazari: I have often reflected about you and come to the conclusion that God has some secret design in preserving you, and that He appointed the Sabbath and holy days among the strongest means of preserving your strength and lustre. The nations broke you up and made you their servants on account of your intelligence and purity. They would even have made you their warriors were it not for those festive seasons observed by you with so much conscientiousness, because they originate with God, and are based on such causes as 'Remembrance of the Creation, Remembrance of the exodus from Egypt, and Remembrance of the giving of the Law. These are all divine commands, to observe which you are charged. Had these not been, not one of you would put on a clean garment; you would hold no congregation to remember the law, on account of your everlasting affliction and degradation. Had these not been, you would not enjoy a single day in your lives. Now, however, you are allowed to spend the sixth part of life in rest of body and soul. Even kings are unable to do likewise, as their souls have no respite on their days of rest. If the smallest business calls them on that day to work and stir, they must move and stir, complete rest being denied to them. Had these laws not been, your toil would benefit others, because it would become their prey. Whatever you spend on these days is your profit for this life and the next, because it is spent for the glory of God.

11. The Rebbi: The observant among us fulfils those divine laws, viz. circumcision, Sabbath, holy days, and the accessories included in the divine law. He refrains from forbidden marriages, using mixtures in plants, clothes and animals, keeps the years of release and jubilee, avoids idolatry and its accessories, viz. discovering secrets only accessible by means of the Urim and the Thummim, or dreams. He does not listen to the soothsayer, or astrologer, or magician, augur or necromancer. He keeps the regulations concerning issue, of eating and touching unclean animals and lepers; abstains from partaking of blood and forbidden fat, because they form part of the **five offerings of the Lord**. He observes the sacrifices ordained for intentional and unintentional transgressions; the duty of redeeming the first-born of man and beast. He brings the offerings for every child born to him, and whenever he is purged from issue and leprosy; pays the various kinds of tithes, visits the Holy Land three times in the year; observes the rules of the Paschal lamb with all accessories, as it is a sacrifice of the Lord incumbent upon every freeborn Israelite. He observes the laws of the tabernacle, the palm branch and Shofar, and takes care of the holy and pure implements required for the offerings. He observes the sacrifices for his own purification, as also the regulation of the corner, the **Orlah**, and the fruits holy to praise the Lord therewith. In short, he observes as many of the divine commands as to justify him in saying: I have not transgressed one of Thy commands, nor forgotten. There are further to be added vows and free gifts, peace offerings and self-denials. These are the religious laws, most of which are performed in connexion with the priestly service. The social laws are such as the following: Thou shalt not murder, thou shalt not commit adultery, steal, give false testimony against thy neighbour, honouring thy parents, you shall love the stranger, you shall not speak untruth and not lie; such as concern the avoidance of usury, the giving of correct weights and measures; the gleanings to be left, such as the forgotten grapes, the corners, etc. The ethical laws are: I am the Lord thy God, thou shalt have no other God, and Thou shalt not take the name of thy God in vain, with its corollary that God is all present, and penetrates all the secrets of man, as well as his actions and words, that he requites good and evil, and that the eyes of the Lord run to and fro, etc. The religious person never acts, speaks or thinks without believing that he is observed by eyes which see and take note, which reward and punish and call to account for everything objectionable in word and deed. In walking or sitting he is like one afraid and timid, who is at times ashamed of his doings; but on the other hand, he is glad and rejoices, and his soul exults whenever he has done a good action, as if he had shown some attention to the Lord in enduring hardships in obedience to God. Altogether he believes in and bears in mind the following words: Consider three things, and thou wilt commit no sin; understand what is above thee, an all-seeing eye and a hearing ear, and all thine actions are written in a book. He further recalls the convincing proof adduced by David: 'He that planted the ear, shall He not hear; He that formed the eye, shall He not, see. There is also the Psalm beginning: O Lord, thou hast searched me and knowest me. When reading it, he remembers that all his limbs are

Kuzari — Third Essay

placed with consummate wisdom, in proper order and proportion. He sees how they obey his will, though he knows not which part of them should move. If, for example, he wishes to rise, he finds that his limbs have, like obedient helpers, raised his body, although he does not even know the nature of these limbs. It is the same when he wishes to sit, walk, or assumes any position. This is expressed in the words: Thou knowest my down sitting and mine uprising... Thou searchest out my path and my lying down, and art acquainted with all my ways. The organs of speech are much finer and more delicate than these. The child, as thou seest, repeats everything he hears, without knowing with which organ, nerve, muscle he must speak. The same is the case with the organs of breathing in singing melodies. People reproduce them quite harmoniously without being aware how it was done; as if their Creator produced them ever anew and placed them in man's service. Such, indeed, is the case; at least it nearly approaches it. One must not consider the work of creation in the light of an artisan's craft. When the latter, has built a mill, he departs, whilst the mill does the work for which it was constructed. The Creator, however, creates limbs and endows them continually with their faculties. Let us imagine His solicitude and guidance removed only for one instant, and the whole world would suffer. If the religious person remembers this with every movement, he first acknowledges the Creator's part in them, for having created and equipped them with the assistance necessary for their permanent perfection. This is as if the Divine Presence were with him continually, and the angels virtually accompanied him. If his piety is consistent, and he abides in places worthy of the Divine Presence, they are with Him in reality, and he sees them with his own eyes occupying a degree just below that of prophecy. Thus, the most prominent of the Sages, during the time of the Second Temple, saw a certain apparition and heard a kind of voice **Bath Qol** [Voice from Heaven] This is the degree of the pious, next to which is that of prophets The pious man derives from his veneration of the Divine Influence, near to him, what the servant derives from his master who created him, loaded him with gifts, and watches him in order to reward or to punish him. Thou wilt not, then, find any exaggeration in the words he utters when retiring into a private chamber: With your permission, O honoured ones, in reference to the Divine Presence! And when he returns, he recites the blessing: 'He that has created man in wisdom.' How sublime is this formula of blessing; what deep meaning is in its wording for him who considers it in the right spirit? Beginning with **wisdom** and concluding with the words: Healer of all flesh and doer of wonders, it furnishes a proof for the miraculous **Ness** visible in the creation of living beings, endowed with the faculties of expelling and retaining. The words 'all flesh' encompass all living beings. In this way he connects his mind with the Divine Influence by various means, some of which are prescribed in the written Law, others in tradition. He wears the phylacteries on his head on the seat of the mind and memory, the straps falling down on his hand, where he can see them at leisure. The hand phylactery he wears above the mainspring of his faculties, the heart. He wears the Zizith lest he be entrapped by worldly thoughts, as it is written: That ye may not go astray after your heart and after your eyes. Inside the phylacteries are written verses describing His unity, reward, punishment, and the remembrance of the exodus from Egypt, because they furnish the irrefutable proof that the Divine Influence is attached to mankind, and that Providence watches them and keeps record of their deeds. The pious man, then, examines his sensations, and devotes part of them to God. Tradition teaches that the smallest measure of praise which it is man's duty to offer to God, consists in a hundred blessings daily. First among these are the ordinary ones, then he supplements them in the course of the day by the blessings which accompany the savouring of odours, eatables and things heard and seen. Whatever he does beyond those is a gain, and brings him nearer to God, as David says: My mouth shall show

Kuzari   Third Essay

forth Thy righteousness, thy salvation all the day, for I know not the numbers thereof. He means to say: Thy glory is not comprehended by numbers, but I will devote myself to it all my life and never be free from it. Love and fear no doubt enter the soul by these means, and are measured with the measure of the law, lest the joy felt on Sabbaths and holy days outstep its bounds and develop into extravagance, debauchery and idleness, and neglect of the hours of prayer. Fear, on the other hand, should not go so far as to despair of forgiveness, and make him spend all his life in dread, causing him to transgress the command given him to feel pleasure in all that sustains him, as it is written: Thou shalt rejoice in every good thing. It would also diminish his gratitude for God's bounties; for gratitude is the effect of joy. He, however, will be as one alluded to in the words: Because thou didst not serve the Lord thy God in joy…. thou shalt serve thine enemies. Zeal in reproving 'thy neighbour, and in study should not pass into wrath and hatred, disturbing the purity of his soul during prayer. He is deeply convinced of the - justice of God's judgment. He finds in its protection and solace from sorrow and the troubles of life if he is convinced of the justice of the Creator of all living creatures; He who sustains and guides them with a wisdom which the human intellect is only capable of grasping in a general way, but not in detail. See how wonderfully conceived is the nature of the creatures; how many marvellous gifts they possess which show forth the intention of an all-wise Creator, and the will of an omniscient all-powerful Being. He has endowed the small and the great with all necessary internal and external senses and limbs. He gave them organs corresponding to their instincts. He gave the hare and stag the means of flight required by their timid nature; endowed the lion with ferocity and the instruments for robbing and tearing. He who considers the formation, use and relation of the limbs to the animal instinct, sees wisdom in them and so perfect an arrangement that no doubt or uncertainty can remain in his soul concerning the justice of the Creator. When an evil thought suggests that there is injustice in the circumstance that the hare falls a prey to the lion or wolf, and the fly to the spider, Reason steps in warning him as follows: How can I charge the all-Wise with injustice when I am convinced of His justice, and that injustice is quite out of the question? If the lion's pursuit of the hare and the spiders of the fly were mere accidents, I should assert the necessity of accident. I see, however, that this wise and just Manager of the world equipped the lion with the means for hunting, with ferocity, strength, teeth and claws; that He furnished the spider with cunning and taught it to weave a net which it constructs without having learnt to do so; how He equipped it with the instruments required, and appointed the fly as its food, just as many fishes serve other fishes for food. Can I say aught but that this is the fruit of a wisdom which I am unable to grasp, and that I must submit to Him who is called: The Rock whose doing is perfect. Whoever reflects on this will do as did Nahum of Gimzo, of whom it is related that no matter what happened to him, he always said: 'This, too, is for the best.' He will, then, always live happily, and all tribulations will fall lightly upon him. He will even welcome them if he is conscious of having transgressed, and will be cleansed through them as one who has paid his debt, and is glad of having eased his mind. He looks joyfully forward to the reward and retribution which await him; nay, he enjoys affording mankind a lesson of patience and submission to God, not less than gaining a good reputation. Thus, it is with his own troubles, and also with those of mankind at large. If his mind is disturbed by the length of the exile and the diaspora and degradation of his people, he finds comfort first in 'acknowledging the justice of the decree, as said before; then in being cleansed from his sins; then in the reward and recompense awaiting him in the world to come, and the attachment to the Divine Influence in this world. If an evil thought makes him despair of it, saying: Can these bones live - our traces being thoroughly destroyed and our history decayed, as it is written: they say: 'our bones are dried - let him think of the manner of the delivery from Egypt and all that is put down in the paragraph: For how many favours do we owe gratitude to God, He will, then, find no difficulty in picturing how we may recover our greatness, though only one of us may have remained. For it is written: Worm of Yaakov - what can remain of a man when he has become a worm in his grave.

12. Al Khazari: In this manner he lives a happy life even in exile; he gathers the fruit of his faith in this world and the next. He, however, who bears the exile unwillingly, loses his first and his last rewards.

13. The Rebbi: His pleasure is strengthened and "Can these bones live?" enhanced by the duty of saying blessings over everything he enjoys or which happens to him in this world.

14. Al Khazari: How can that be, are not the blessings an additional burden.

15. The Rebbi: Is it not beseeming that a perfect man should find more pleasure in that which he partakes than a child or an animal; even as an animal enjoys it more than does a plant though the latter is continually taking nourishment.

16. Al Khazari: This is so because he is

favoured with the consciousness of enjoyment. If a drunken person were given all he desires, whilst being completely intoxicated, he would eat and drink, hear songs, meet his friends, and embrace his beloved. But if told of it when sober, he would regret it and regard it as a loss rather than a gain, since he had all these enjoyments whilst he was incapable of appreciating them.

17. The Rebbi: Preparing for a pleasure, experiencing it and looking forward to it, double the feeling of enjoyment. This is the advantage of the blessings for him who is used to say them with attention and devotion. They produce in his soul a kind of pleasure and gratitude towards the Giver. He was prepared to give them up; now his pleasure is all the greater, and he says: He has kept us alive and preserved us. He was prepared for death, now he feels gratitude for life, and regards it as gain. Should sickness and death overtake thee, they will be light, because thou hast communed with thyself and seen that thou gainest with thy Lord. According to thy nature thou art well fitted to abjure enjoyment, since thou art dust. Now he has presented thee with life and desire; thou art grateful to Him. If He takes them away, thou sayest: The Lord has given, the Lord has taken. Thus, thy whole life is one enjoyment. Whoever is unable to pursue such a course, consider not his pleasure a human pleasure, but a brutish one, which he does not perceive, any more than the drunkard alluded to above. The godly person fully grasps the meaning of each blessing, and knows its purpose in every connexion. The blessing, He who created the lights, places before his eye the order of the upper world, the greatness of the heavenly bodies and their usefulness, that in the eyes of their Creator they are no greater than worms, though they appear to us immense on account of the profit we derive from them. The proof that He is their Creator may be found in the circumstance already mentioned, that His wisdom and power observable in the creation of the ant and bee is not less than in that of the sun and its sphere. The traces of this providence and wisdom are finer and more wonderful in the ant and bee, because, in spite of their minuteness, He put faculties and organs into them. This he bears in mind lest the light appear to him too great, and an evil genius lead him to adopt some views of worshippers of spirits, and make him believe that the sun and moon are able to help or injure independently, whilst they can only assist to do so indirectly, like the wind and fire. It is written: If I behold the sun when it shines…. and my heart has been secretly enticed. At the blessing beginning: with eternal love, he, in a similar manner, bears in mind the attachment of the Divine Influence to the community which was prepared to receive it, as a smooth mirror

Kuzari — Third Essay

receives the light, and that the Law is the outcome of His will in order to establish His sway on earth; as it is in heaven. His wisdom did not demand of Him to create angels on earth, but mortals of flesh and blood, in whom natural gifts and certain characteristics prevail according to favourable or unfavourable influences, as this is explained in the Book of Creation. Whenever some few, or a whole community, are sufficiently pure, the divine light rests on them and guides in an incomprehensible and miraculous manner which is quite outside the ordinary course of the natural world. This is called 'Love and joy." The Divine Influence, however, found next to the stars and spheres none who accepted his commands and who adhered to the course He had dictated, with the exception of a few between Adam and Yaakov. When they had become a people, the Divine Influence rested upon them out of love, 'in order to be a God unto them.' In the desert he arranged them in the manner of the sphere in four standards, corresponding to the four quarters of the sphere, and in twelve tribes, corresponding to the twelve signs of the zodiac, the camp of the Levites being in the centre, just as it is stated in the Book of Creation. The holy Temple is exactly in the centre, but God carries them all. All this points to **love** for the sake of which the blessing is recited. In the reading of the Shema, which then follows, he accepts the obligations of the Law, as in the piece beginning **True and certain, which expresses the firm resolution to observe the Torah**. This is as if, after having clearly and unmistakably imbibed all that preceded, he binds his soul and testifies that the children should submit to the Law for ever, just as the forefathers had done, according to the words: 'Upon our fathers, and upon us, and our children and our coming generations... a good word, firmly established, that never passes away.' To this he attaches these articles of creed which complete the Jewish belief, viz. the recognition of God's sovereignty, His eternity, and the providential care which He bestowed on our forefathers; that the Torah emanated from Him, and that the proof for all this is to be found in the delivery from Egypt. This is alluded to in the words: 'It is true that Thou art the Lord our God; truly from everlasting is Thy name... the help of our fathers... from Egypt didst Thou redeem us.' He who unites all this in pure thought is a true Israelite and worthy of aspiring to the Divine Influence which among all nations was exclusively connected with the children of Israel. He finds no difficulty in standing before the Divine Presence, and he receives an answer as often as he asks. The prayer of the 'Eighteen Benedictions' must follow the blessing 'He has redeemed Israel' immediately and promptly, standing upright for this prayer in the condition described previously, when we discussed the blessings which relate to the whole Israelitish nation. Prayers of more individual character are voluntary and not incumbent, and they have their place in the paragraph ending, He who hears the prayer. In the first paragraph, entitled, **Fathers**, the worshipper remembers the piety of the Patriarchs, the establishment of the covenant with them on the part of God for all times, which never ceases, as is expressed in the words: He brings the Redeemer to their children's children. The second blessing, known as **Mighty Deeds**, teaches that God's is the eternal rule of the world, not however, as natural philosophers assert, that this is done by natural and empirical means. The worshipper is further reminded that He revives the dead' whenever He desires, however far this may be removed from the speculation of natural philosophers. Similar ideas prevail in the words: He causes the wind to blow, and the rain to descend. According to His desire He delivers those in bondage, as may be established by instances from the history of Israel. Having read these paragraphs which enlighten him in the belief that God keeps up a connexion with this material world, the worshipper extols and sanctifies Him by the declaration that no corporeal attitude appertains to Him. This is done in the paragraph beginning: 'Thou art holy,' a blessing which inculcates belief in the attributes of sublimity and holiness commented upon by philosophers. This paragraph follows the others in which the absoluteness of God's sovereignty is laid down. They convince us that we have a King and Lawgiver, and without them we had lived in doubt, the theories of philosophers and materialists. The paragraphs of 'Fathers' and **Mighty Deeds**, must therefore precede that of the **sanctification of God**. After this the worshipper begins to pray for the wants of the whole of Israel, and it is not permissible to insert other prayers except in the place of voluntary supplications. A prayer, in order to be heard, must be recited for a multitude, or in a multitude or, for an individual who could take the place of a multitude. None such, however, is to be found in our age.

18. Al Khazari: Why is this? If every one read his prayers for himself, would not his soul be purer and his mind less abstracted.

19. The Rebbi: Common prayer has many advantages. In the first instance a community will never pray for a thing which is hurtful for the individual, whilst the latter sometimes prays for something, to the disadvantage of other individuals, or some of them may pray for something, that is to his disadvantage. One of the conditions of prayer, craving to be heard, is that its object be profitable to the world, but not hurtful in any way. Another is that an individual rarely accomplishes his prayer without slips and errors. It has been laid down, therefore, that the individual recites the prayers of a community, and if possible, in a community of not less than ten persons, so that one makes up for the forgetfulness or error of the other. In this way, a complete prayer is gained, read with unalloyed devotion. Its blessing rests on everyone, each receiving his portion. For the Divine Influence is as the rain which waters an area if deserving of it, and includes some smaller portion which does not deserve it, but shares the general abundance. On the other hand, the rain is withheld from an area which does not deserve it, although some portion is included which did deserve it, but suffers with the majority. This is how God governs the world. He reserves the reward of every individual for the world to come; but in this world He gives him the best compensation, granting salvation in contradiction to His neighbours. There are but few who completely escape the general retribution. A person who prays but for himself is like him who retires alone into his house, refusing to assist his fellow-citizens in the repair of their walls. His expenditure is as great as his risk. He, however, who joins the majority spends little, yet remains in safety, because one replaces the defects of the other. The city is in the best possible condition, all its inhabitants enjoying its prosperity with but little expenditure, which all share alike. In a similar manner, Plato styles that which is expended on behalf of the law, the portion of the whole. If the individual, however, neglects this 'portion of the whole' which is the basis of the welfare of the commonwealth of which he forms a part, in the belief that he does better in spending it on himself, sins against the commonwealth, and more against himself. For the relation of the individual is as the relation of the single limb to the body. Should the arm, in case bleeding is required, refuse its blood, the whole body, the arm included, would suffer. It is, however, the duty of the individual to bear hardships, or even death, for the sake of the welfare of the commonwealth. He must particularly be careful to contribute his **portion of the whole**, without fail. Since ordinary speculation did not institute this, God prescribed it in tithes, gifts, and offerings, etc., as a portion of the whole of worldly property. Among actions this is represented by Sabbath, holy days, years of release and jubilee and similar institutions; among words it is prayers, blessings and thanksgivings; among abstract things it is love, fear and joy. The first place of the second group of blessings is very appropriately given to the prayer for intelligence and enlightenment to obey God. Man prays to be brought near to his Master. He, therefore, says first: 'Thou graciously givest reason to man, which is immediately followed by 'He who takes delight in repentance. Thus wisdom, knowledge and intelligence move in the path of the Law and worship in the words: Restore us, O our Father, to Thy Law. Since mortal man cannot help sinning, a prayer is required for forgiveness of transgressions in thought and deed. This is done in the formula ending: the Merciful who forgiveth much. To this paragraph he adds the result and sign of forgiveness, viz. the redemption from our present condition. He begins: **Behold our misery**, and concludes: 'Redeemer of Israel. After this he prays for the health of body and soul, and for the bestowal of food to keep up the strength in the blessing of the years. Then he prays for the reunion of the scattered, in the paragraph ending: He who gathers together the scattered of His people of the house of Israel. With this is connected the re-appearance of justice and restoration of the former condition of the people in the words: Rule over us Thou alone. He, then, prays against evil and the destruction of the thorns in the paragraph of the 'heretics.' This is followed by the prayer for the preservation of the pure essence in: **The just**. He, then, prays for the return to Jerusalem which again is to form the seat of the Divine Influence, and with this is connected the prayer concerning the MASHIACH, the son of David. This concludes all worldly wants. He now prays for the acceptance of his prayer, as well as for the visible revelation of the Shekhinah, just as appeared to the prophets, pious, and those who were delivered from Egypt, in the paragraph ending: O Thou who hearest prayer. Then he prays: Let mine eye behold, and concludes: He who restores His Shekhinah to Zion. He imagines the Shekhinah standing opposite to him and bows down with the words: 'We give thanks,' which contain the acknowledgment and gratitude for God's mercy. The whole concludes with the paragraph: **He maketh peace**, in order to take leave from the Shekhinah in peace.

20. Al Khazari: There is nothing to criticise, as I see how settled and circumspect all these arrangements are. There was one point to be mentioned, viz. that your prayers say so little of the world to come. But thou hast already proved to me that he who prays for attachment to the Divine Light, and the faculty of seeing it with his own eyes in this world, and who, nearly approaching the rank of prophets, is thus engaged in prayer-and nothing can bring man nearer to God than this-has without doubt prayed for more than the world to come. He gains it with the other. He whose soul is in contact with the Divine Influence, though still exposed to the accidents and sufferings of the body, it stands to reason that it will gain a more intimate connexion with the former, when it has become free and detached from this unclean vessel.

21. The Rebbi: I can explain this better to thee by a parable. A man visited the king. The latter accorded him his most intimate friendship, and permitted him to enter his presence whenever he wished. He became so familiar with the king that he invited him to his house and table. The king not only consented, but sent his noblest veziers to him and did to him what he had done to no one else. Whenever he had neglected something, or had done something wrong, and the king kept aloof from him, he only entreated him to return to his former custom, and not to forbid his veziers to come and see him. The other inhabitants of the country only craved the king's protection when they undertook a journey, against robbers, wild beasts, and the terrors of the road. They were confident that the king would assist and take care of them during their journey, although he had never done so as long as they remained at home. Each of them boasted that the king cared for him more than for anybody else, thinking he had honoured the king more than anybody else. The stranger, however, thought little of his departure, nor did he ask for a guard. When the hour arrived, he was told that he would perish in the dangers of the journey since he had no one to take care of him. Who gave you companions? asked he. **The king** said they, 'whom we have petitioned for assistance ever since we have been in this city;' but we have not seen thee do likewise. **You fool**, answered he; 'is a person who called on him in the hour of safety not more entitled to expect his assistance in the hour of danger, though he did not open his mouth? Will he refuse his assistance to a man in the time of need after having responded to him during his prosperity? If you boast that he takes care of you because you have shown him honour, has anyone of you done so much in this respect, took so much trouble in the execution of his commands, in keeping aloof from dishonour, in respecting his name and code as I did? Whatever I did, I did at his command and instruction. As to you, you honour him according to your own conception and fancy, yet he fails you not. How can he, now, leave me, if I am in need, during my journey, because, trusting his justice, I did not speak to him of it as you have done.' This parable is only meant for those who depart from the right course, and do not accept the words of the Sages. But apart from this, our prayers are full of allusions of the world to come, and the utterances of the Sages, which are handed down from the Prophets, are studded with descriptions of Paradise and Gehinnom, as explained before. Now I have sketched out to thee the conduct of a religious person in the present time, and thou canst imagine what it was like in that happy time and that divine place amidst the people whose roots were Abraham, Itzhak and Yaakov. They represent the essence of the latter, men and women distinguished by virtue, suffering nothing unbecoming to pass their lips. The godly man moves about among them, but his soul is not polluted by the improper words which he may hear, nor does any impurity adhere to his garment or dress from issue, or vermin, or corpses, or leprosy, etc., because they all live in holiness and purity. This is in a greater measure the case in the land of the Shekhinah, where he only meets people who occupy the degree of holiness, as Priest, Levites, Nazirites, Sages, Prophets, Judges and Overseers. Or he sees - a multitude that kept holiday with the voice of joy and praise, on the three festivals in the year. He only hears the 'Song of the Lord,' only sees the 'Work of the Lord,' particularly if he is a priest or Levite who lives on the bread of the Lord and, like Samuel, lives in the 'House of the Lord' from his infancy. He need not seek any livelihood, as his whole life is devoted to the 'Service of the Lord.' How does his work and the purity and excellence of his soul appear to thee.

22. Al Khazari: This is the highest degree, above which there is none but the angelic one. Such a mode of life entitles man to the prophetic afflatus, particularly there where the Shekhinah dwells. A religion of this kind can do without ascetic or monastic retirement. Now I request thee to give me an outline of the doctrine of the Karaites. For I see that they are much more zealous believers than the Rabbanites, and their arguments are, as I perceive, more striking and in harmony with the Torah.

23. The Rebbi: Did we not state before that speculation, reasoning and fiction on the Law do not lead to the pleasure of God? Otherwise, dualists, materialists, worshippers of spirits, anchorites, and those who burn their children are all endeavouring to come near to God? We have, however, said, that one cannot approach God except by His commands. For he knows their comprehensiveness, division, times, and places, and consequences in the fulfilment of which the pleasure of God and the connexion with the Divine Influence are to be gained. Thus, it was in the building of the Tabernacle. With every item it is said: And Bezaleel made the ark..., the lid..., the carpets..., and concerning each of them is stated: Just as the Lord had commanded Moshe. This means neither too much nor too little, although our speculation cannot bear on works of this kind. Finally, it is said: And Moshe saw the whole work, and behold they had performed it just as the Lord had commanded, thus they worked, and Moshe blessed them. The completion of the Tabernacle was followed by the descent of the Shekhinah, the two conditions which form the pillars of the Law having been fulfilled, viz., firstly, that the Law originated with God;

secondly, that the people conformed with it in a pure mind. God commanded the building of the Tabernacle, and the whole people obeyed- as it is said: Of every man that giveth it willingly with his heart, shall ye take My offering - with the greatest zeal and enthusiasm. The result was equally perfect, viz. the appearance of the Shekhinah, as it is said: And I will dwell in their midst. I gave thee the example of the creation of the plant and animal, and told thee that the form which distinguishes one plant from another and one animal from another is not a natural force but a work of God, called nature by philosophers. As a matter of fact, the powers of nature are capable of favouring such a development according to the proportion of heat and cold, moisture and dryness. One thing would, then, become a plant, another a vine, this a horse, that a lion. We are unable to determine these proportions, and could we do it, we might produce blood or milk, etc. from liquids mixed by our own calculations. We might, eventually, create living beings, endowed with the spirit of life. Or we might produce a substitute for bread from ingredients which have no nourishing powers, simply by mixing the right proportions of heat and cold, moisture and dryness, and particularly if we knew the spherical constellations and their influences which, in the opinion of astrologers, assist to bring forth of anything that is desired in this world. We have seen, however, that all alchymists and necromancers who have tried those things, have been put to shame. Do not raise the objection that these people are able to produce animals and living beings, as bees from flesh and gnats from wine. These are not the consequences of their calculations and agency, but of experiments. It was found that cohabitation was followed by the birth of a child; man, however, does but plant the seed in the soil prepared to receive and develop it. The calculation of proportions which give the human form belongs exclusively to the Creator. In the same manner is the determination of the living people worthy to form the seat of the Divine Influence God's alone. This calculating and weighing, must be learnt from Him, but we should not reason about His word, as it is written: There is no wisdom nor understanding nor counsel against the Lord. What dost thou think we should adopt in order to become like our fathers, to imitate them, and not to speculate about the Law.

24. Al Khazari: We can only accomplish this through the medium of their traditional teachings, by the support of their deeds, and by endeavouring to find one who is regarded as an authority by one generation, and capable of handing down the history of another. The latter generation, however, cannot, on account of the multitude of its individuals, be suspected of having made a general agreement to carry the Law with its branches and interpretations unaltered from Moshe downward either in their memories or in a volume.

25. The Rebbi: And what will you say if he finds a replacement in one book or in two and three.

26. Al Khazari: What wouldst thou think if difference were found in one or two copies.

27. The Rebbi: One must study several copies, the majority of which cannot be faulty. The minority can, then, be neglected. The same process applies to traditions. If the minority differs, we turn to the majority.

28. Al Khazari: Now, what is thy opinion if in the manuscripts a letter were found which is in contrast to common sense. ṣadu, where we should expect ṣaru, and nafshi, where we should read nafsho.

29. The Rebbi: In which form did Moshe leave his book to the Israelites in thy opinion.

30. Al Khazari: Common sense would in these and other cases alter in all volumes, first the letters, then the words, then the construction, then the vowels and accents, and consequently also the sense. There are many verses to which the reader can give an opposite meaning by altering the place of any of these appositives.

31. The Rebbi: Undoubtedly without either vowels or accents, just as our scrolls are written. There was as little agreement possible among the people on this point, as on the unleavened bread, or Passover, or other laws which were given as a remembrance of the delivery from Egypt. These laws confirm in the minds of the Israelites the historical truth of the exodus from Egypt by means of the recurring ceremonies, which could not possibly be the result of common agreement without causing contradiction. There is, therefore, no doubt that the Book was preserved in memory with all its vowels, divisions of syllables and accents: by the priests, because they required them for the Temple service, and in order to teach the people; by the kings, because they were commanded: And it shall be with him and he shall read therein all the days of his life. The judges had to know it to enable them to give judgment; the members of the Sanhedrion, because they were warned: Keep therefore and do them, for this is your wisdom and understanding; the pious, in order to receive reward; and, finally, the hypocrites, to acquire a good name. The seven vowels and accents were appointed as signs for forms which were regarded as Mosaic tradition. Now, how have we to judge those persons who first divided the text into verses, equipped it with vowel signs, accents, and masoretic signs, concerning full or defective orthography; and counted the letters with such accuracy that they found out that the gimel of gaḥon. Stood right in the middle of the Torah, and kept a record of all irregular vowels. Dost, thou consider this work either superfluous or idle, or dutiful zeal.

32. Al Khazari: The latter no doubt. It was to serve as a fence round the law in order to leave no room for alterations. Moreover, it is a great science. The system of vowel signs and accents reveals an order which could only emanate from divinely-instilled notions, quite out of proportion to our knowledge. It can only have been received from a community of favoured ones or a single individual of the same stamp. In the latter case it must have been a prophet, or a person assisted by the Divine Influence. For a scholar who lacks this assistance can be challenged by another scholar to adopt his views in preference.

33. The Rebbi: The acknowledgment of tradition is therefore incumbent upon us as well as upon the Karaites, as upon anyone who admits that the Torah, in its present shape and as it is read, is the Torah of Moshe.

34. Al Khazari: This is exactly what the Karaites say. But as they have the complete

Torah, they consider the tradition superfluous.

35. The Rebbi: Far from it. If the consonantic text of the Mosaic Book requires so many traditional classes of vowel signs, accents, divisions of sentences and masoretic signs for the correct pronunciation of words, how much more is this the case for the comprehension of the same? The meaning of a word is more comprehensive than its pronunciation. When God revealed the verse: This month shall be unto you the beginning of months, there was no doubt whether He meant the calendar of the Copts-or rather the Egyptians-among whom they lived, or that of the Chaldaeans who were Avraham's people in Ur-Kasdim; or solar or lunar months, or lunar years, which are made to agree with solar years, as is done in embolismic years. I wish the Karaites could give me a satisfactory answer to questions of this kind. I would not hesitate to adopt their view, as it pleases me to be enlightened. I further wish to be instructed on the question as to what makes an animal lawful for food; whether 'slaughtering' means cutting its throat or any other mode of killing; why killing by gentiles makes the flesh unlawful; what is the difference between slaughtering, skinning, and the rest of it. I should desire an explanation of the forbidden fat, seeing that it lies in the stomach and entrails close to the lawful fat, as well as of the rules of cleansing the meat. Let them draw me the line between the fat which is lawful and that which is not, inasmuch as there is no difference visible. Let them explain to me where the tail of the sheep, which they declare unlawful, ends. One of them may possibly forbid the end of the tail alone, another the whole hind part. I desire an explanation of the lawful and unlawful birds, excepting the common ones, such as the pigeon and turtle dove. How do they know that the hen, goose, duck, and partridge are not unclean birds? I further desire an explanation of the words: Let no man go out of his place on the seventh day. Does this refer to the house or precincts, estate - where he can have many houses-territory, district, or country. For the word place can refer to all of these. I should, further, like to know where the prohibition of work on the Sabbath commences? Why pens and writing material are not admissible in the correction of a scroll of the Law on this day, but lifting a heavy book, or a table, or eatables, entertaining guests and all cares of hospitality should be permitted, although the guests would be resting, and the host be kept employed? This applies even more to women and servants, as it is written: That thy manservant and thy maidservant rest as well as thou. Wherefore it is forbidden to ride on the Sabbath horses belonging to gentiles, or to trade. Then, again, I wish to see a Karaite give judgment between two parties according to the chapters. For that which appears plain in the Torah, is yet obscure, and much more so are the obscure passages, because the oral supplement was relied upon. I should wish to hear the deductions he draws from the case of the daughters of Zelophehad to questions of inheritance in general. I want to know the details of circumcision, fringes and tabernacle; why it is incumbent on him to say prayers; whence he derives his belief in reward and punishment in the world after death; how to deal with laws which interfere with each other, as circumcision or Paschal lamb with Sabbath, which must yield to which, and many other matters which cannot be enumerated in general, much less in detail. Hast thou ever heard, O King of the Khazars, that the Karaites possess a book which contains a fixed tradition on one of the subjects just mentioned, and which allows no differences on readings, vowel signs, accents, or lawful or unlawful matters, or decisions.

36. Al Khazari: I have neither seen anything of the kind, nor heard about it. I see, nevertheless, that they are very zealous.

37. The Rebbi: This, as I have already told thee, belongs in the province of speculative theory. Those who speculate on the ways of glorifying God for the purpose of His worship, are much more zealous than those who practise the service of God exactly as it is commanded. The latter are at ease with their tradition, and their soul is calm like one who lives in a town, and they fear not any hostile opposition. The former, however, is like a straggler in the desert, who does not know what may happen. He must provide himself with arms and prepare for battle like one expert in warfare. Be not, therefore, astonished to see them so energetic, and do not lose courage if thou seest the followers of tradition, I mean the Rabbanites, falter. The former look for a fortress where they can entrench themselves, whilst the latter lie down on their couches in a place well fortified of old.

38. Al Khazari: All thou sayest is convincing, because the Law enjoins that there shall be one Torah and one statute. Should Karaite methods prevail there would be as many different codes as opinions. Not one individual would remain constant to one code. For every day he forms new opinions, increases his knowledge, or meets with someone who refutes him with some argument and converts him to his views. But whenever we find them agreeing, we know that they follow the tradition of one or many of their ancestors. In such a case we should not believe their views, and say: How is it that you agree concerning this regulation, whilst reason allows the word of God to be interpreted in various ways. If the answer be that this was the opinion of Anan, or Benjamin, Saul, or others, then they admit the authority of tradition received from people who lived before them, and of the best tradition, viz. that of the Sages. For they were many, whilst those Karaite teachers were but single individuals. The view of the Rebbis is based on the tradition of the Prophets; the other, however, on speculation alone. The Sages are in concord, the Karaites in discord. The sayings of the Sages originate with 'the place which God shall choose,' and we must therefore accept even their individual opinions. The Karaites have nothing of the kind. I wish I knew their answer regarding the calculation of the new moon I see that their authorities follow Rabbanite practice in the intercalation of Adar. Nevertheless, they taunt the Rabbanites, when the Tishri new moon appears, with the question: 'How could it happen that you once kept the fast of the day of Atonement on the ninth of Tishri?' Are they not ashamed not to know, when intercalating, whether the month is Ellul or Tishri; or Tishri or Marḥeshwan, if they do not intercalate? They ought rather to say: 'I am drowning, but fear not the wet!' We do not know whether the month is Tishri, Marḥeshwan, or Ellul. How can we criticise those in whose steps we follow, and whose teachings we adopt, and ask: Do you fast on the ninth or tenth of Tishri.

39. The Rebbi: Our law is linked to the ordination given to Moshe on Sinai, or sprung from the place which the Lord shall choose, for from Zion goes forth the Law, and the word of God from Jerusalem. Its mediators were the Judges, Overseers, Priests, and the members of the Synhedrion. It is incumbent upon us to obey the Judge appointed for the time being, as it is written: Or to the judge who will be in those days... and thou shalt inquire, and they shall tell thee the sentence of judgment, and thou shalt do according to the word which they tell thee... from the place which the Lord shall choose... and thou shall take heed to do according to all they teach thee. Further: The man who doeth presumptuously not to listen to the priest... this man shall die, and thou shalt remove the evil from thy midst. Disobedience to the Priest or Judge is placed on a par with the gravest transgressions, in the words: Thou shalt remove the evil from thy midst. This concludes with the words: And all the people shall hear and fear, and do no more presumptuously.' This refers to the time when the order of the Temple service and the Synhedrion, and the sections of the Levites, who completed the organization, were still intact, and the Divine Influence was undeniably among them either in the form of prophecy or inspiration, as was the case during the time of the second Temple. Among these persons no agreement or convention was possible. In a similar manner arose the duty of reading the Book of Esther on Purim, and the ordination of Ḥanuccah, and we can say: 'He who has commanded us to read the Megillah and to kindle the light of Ḥanuccah, or to complete or to read the Hallel, to wash the hands, the ordination of the Erub, and the like. Had our traditional customs arisen after the exile, they could not have been called by this name, nor would they require a blessing, but there would be a regulation or rather a custom. The bulk of our laws, however, derives its origin from Moshe, as an 'ordination given to Moshe from Sinai.' This also explains how a people obtained during forty years sufficient food and clothing, in spite of their large number. Moshe was with them, and the Shekhinah did not forsake them, giving them general as well as special laws. Is it not absurd to assume that they refrained from inquiring occasionally into the details, and handing down their explanations and subdivisions? Take the verse: And I will make known the laws of God and His statutes, which is supplemented by the other: For this is your wisdom and understanding in the eyes of the nations, which shall hear all these laws, and they will say, surely this great nation is a wise and understanding people. He who wishes to gainsay this verse may look at the Karaites; but he who desires to confirm it, let him behold the branches of knowledge embodied in the Talmud, which form only a small portion of the

Kuzari — Third Essay

natural, metaphysical, mathematical, and astronomical studies in which the Sages indulged. He will, then, see that they deserve praise above all nations for their learning. Some of our laws originate, in certain circumstances mentioned before, 'from the place which the Lord shall choose.' Prophecy lasted about forty years of the second Temple. Jeremiah, in his prophetic speeches, commended the people of the second Temple for their piety, learning, and fear of God. If we did not rely on men like these, on whom should we rely? We see those prescriptions given after Moshe' death became law. Thus, Shlomo hallowed: The middle of the court, slaughtered sacrifices on a place other than the altar, and celebrated the feast seven days and seven days. David and Samuel appointed the order of the Temple choir, which became a fixed law. Shlomo added to the sanctuary built in the desert, and omitted from it. Ezra imposed the tax of one-third of a shekel on the community of the second Temple. A stone paving was put in the place of the Ark, hiding it behind a curtain, because they knew that the Ark had been buried there.

40. Al Khazari: How could this be made to agree with the verse: Thou shalt not add thereto, nor diminish from it.

41. The Rebbi: This was only said to the

masses, that they should not conjecture and theorise, and contrive laws according to their own conception, as the Karaites do. They were recommended to listen to the post-Mosaic prophets, the priests and judges, as it is written: I will raise them up a prophet... and he shall speak unto them all that I shall command him. With regard to the priests and judges it is said that their decisions are binding. The words: You shall not add, etc., refer to that which I commanded you through Moshe and any prophet from among thy brethren, who fulfils the conditions of a prophet. They further refer to regulations laid down in common by priests and judges from the place which thy Lord shall choose. For they have divine assistance, and would never, on account of their large number, concur in anything which contradicts the Law. Much less likelihood was there of erroneous views, because they had inherited vast learning, for the reception of which they were naturally endowed. The members of the Synhedrion, as is known by tradition, had to possess a thorough acquaintance with all branches of science Prophecy had scarcely ceased, or rather the **Bath Qol** [Voice from Heaven], which took its place. Now, suppose we allow the Karaite interpretation of the sentence from the morrow of the Sabbath till the morrow of the Sabbath, to refer to the Sunday. But we reply that one of the judges, priests, or pious kings, in agreement with the

Synhedrion and all Sages, found that this period was fixed with the intention of creating an interval of fifty days between 'the first fruits of the harvest of barley and the harvest of wheat, and to observe **seven weeks**, which are seven complete Sabbaths. The first day of the week is only mentioned for argument's sake in the following manner: should the day of putting the sickle to the corn be a Sunday, you count till Sunday. From this we conclude that should the beginning be on a Monday; we count till Monday. The date of putting the sickle, from which we count, is left for us to fix. This was fixed for the second day of Passover, which does not contradict the Torah, since it originated with the place which the Lord shall choose on the conditions discussed before. Perhaps this was done under the influence of divine inspiration. It was quite possible, and it saves us from the confusion of those who endeavour to cause confusion.

42. Al Khazari: With these broad and irrefutable declarations thou hast cut off, O Rebbi, some minor points which I had in my mind to urge on behalf of the Karaite interpretation, by which I hoped to silence thee.

43. The Rebbi: If the general principles are obvious to thee do not mind minor details. The latter are often subject to error, and owing to their wide ramification, know no bounds, and lead astray those who regard them from different points of view. A person who is convinced of the justice of the Creator and His all-embracing wisdom will pay no attention to apparent cases of injustice on earth, as it is written: If thou seest the oppression of the poor and violent perverting of judgment and justice in a province, marvel not at the matter. Whoever is convinced of the duration of the soul after the destruction of the body, as well as of its incorporeal nature and of its being as far removed from corporeality as the angels are, will pay no attention to the idea that the activity of the soul is stopped during sleep or illness which submerges the mental powers, that it is subject to the vicissitudes of the body, and similar disquieting ideas.

44. Al Khazari: Yet I am not satisfied as long as I leave those details undiscussed, though I have admitted those general principles.

45. The Rebbi: Say what thou wilt.

46. Al Khazari: Does not our Torah teach retaliation, viz. **eye for eye**, tooth for tooth, as he hath caused a blemish in man, so shall be done to him.

47. The Rebbi: And is it not said immediately afterwards: And he that killeth a beast shall make it good, life for life. Is this not the principle of ransom? It is not said: If anyone kills thy horse, kill his horse, but 'take his horse, for what use is it to thee to kill his horse, likewise: If anyone has cut off thy hand, take the value of his hand; for cutting off his hand profits thee not. The sentence: Wound for wound and stripe for stripe, embodies ideas antagonistic to common sense. How can we determine such a thing? One person may die from a wound, whilst another person may recover from the same. How can we gauge whether it is the same? How can we take away the eye of a one-eyed person in order to do justice to a person with two eyes, when the former would be totally blind, the latter still have one eye? The Torah teaches: As he hath caused a blemish in man, so shall be done to him. What further need is there to discuss these details, when we have just set forth the necessity of tradition, the truthfulness, loftiness, and religious zeal of traditionists.

48. Al Khazari: For all that, I am surprised that you observe the regulations of religious purity.

49. The Rebbi: Impurity and holiness are contradictory ideas; one cannot be thought of without the other. Without holiness we should not know the signification of impurity. Impurity means that the approach to holy objects, hallowed by God, is forbidden to the

Kuzari — Third Essay

person so affected. Such would be priests, their food, clothing, offering, sacrifices, the holy House, etc. In the same way the ideas of holiness include something which forbids the person connected with it to approach many ordinary objects. This chiefly depends on the vicinity of the Shekhinah, which we now lack entirely. The prohibition which still holds good, of cohabiting with a woman in her period or after confinement has nothing to do with impurity, but is an independent divine law. The practice we observe to keep aloof from them as much as possible is but a restriction and hedge to prevent cohabitation. The regulations of impurity proper ceased to exist for us, because we live in an unclean land and in unclean air, especially as we move about among graves, vermin, lepers, persons affected with issue, corpses, etc. To touch carrion is not forbidden on account of its impurity, but it forms a special law connected with the prohibition of eating the same to which impurity is accessory. If Ezra had not ordained a bath for certain contaminated persons, this would not be a regulation but simply a matter of cleanliness. If these persons would conceive this regulation in the sense of cleanliness, it would lose nothing, as long as it is not taken for a religious law. Otherwise, they might draw conclusions from their own folly, try to improve upon the law and cause heterodoxy, I mean the splitting of opinions, which is the beginning of the corruption of a religion. They would soon be outside the pale of one law and one regulation. Whatever we might allow ourselves in matters of touching even repulsive things, is out of proportion to their, the Karaites schismatic views, which might cause us to find in one house ten persons with as many different opinions. Were our laws not fixed and confined in unbreakable rules, they would not be secure from the intrusion of strange elements and the loss of some component parts, because argument and taste would become guiding principles. The Karaite would have no compunction in using the implements of idolatry, such as gold, silver, frankincense and wine. Indeed, death is better than this. On the other hand, he would abstain from using parts of the pig, even for purposes of medicine, although this is in reality one of the lighter transgressions, and only punished with forty stripes. In the same way he would allow the Nazirite to eat raisins and grapes rather than be intoxicated with mead and cider. But the opposite is true. This prohibition only refers to the products of the vine, but there was no intention of prohibiting intoxication altogether, as one might surmise. This is one of the secrets known only to God, his prophets and the pious. One must not, however, charge traditionists or those who draw their own conclusions, with ignorance in this matter, because the word shekhar is common property. They have a tradition that the wine and strong drink, mentioned in connexion with the priests includes all kinds of intoxication, whilst the same words in the case of the Nazirite only refer to the juice of grapes. Every law has certain limits fixed with scientific accuracy, though in practice they may appear illogical. He who is zealous tries to avoid them, without, however, making them unlawful, as. the flesh of an animal in peril of death, which is lawful. For it is uncertain whether this animal will die, because some one might assert that it will recover, and then be permitted. A diseased animal which externally looks in good health is unlawful, if it suffers internally from an incurable illness, with which it can neither live nor recover. Those who judge according to their own taste and reasoning may arrive in these matters at an opposite conclusion. Follow not, therefore, thy own taste and opinion in religious questions, lest they throw thee into doubts, which lead to heresy. Nor wilt thou be in harmony with one of thy friends on any point. Every individual has his own taste and opinion. It is only necessary to examine the roots of the traditional and written laws with the inferences codified for practice, in order to trace the branches back to the roots. Where they lead thee, there put thy faith, though thy mind and feeling shrink from it. Common view and assumption deny the non-existence of the vacuum, whilst logical conclusion rejects its existence. Appearance denies the infinite divisibility of a body, whilst logic makes it an axiom. Appearance denies that the earth is a globe and the one hundred and sixtieth part of the sun disc. There are also other matters which astronomy establishes against mere appearances. Whatever the Sages declared lawful they did neither in obedience to their own taste or inclination, but to the results of the inherited knowledge, handed down to them. The same was the case with what they declared unlawful. He who is unable to grasp their wisdom, but judges their speech according to his own conception, will misinterpret them in the same way as people do with the words of natural philosophers and astronomers. Whenever they settle the limits of the code, and explain what is lawful or unlawful in strictly juridical deduction, they indicate apparently unseemly points. They consider it revolting to eat the flesh of a dangerously sick animal, or to gain money by means of legal trickery, or to travel on the Sabbath with the assistance of the Erub, or to render certain marriages lawful in a cunning manner, or to undo oaths and vows by circumvention, which may be permitted according to the paragraph of the law, but is devoid of any religious feeling. Both, however, are necessary together, for, if one is guided by the legal deduction alone, more relaxation would crop up than could be controlled. If, on the other hand, one would neglect the legalized lines which form the fence round the law, and would only rely on religious zeal, it would become a source of schism, and destroy everything.

50. Al Khazari: If this be so, I willingly admit that the Rabbanite who unites these two points of view is superior to the Karaite both in theory and practice. He would also perform his religious duties cheerfully, because they are handed down to him by trustworthy authorities who derived their knowledge from God. However far a Karaite's zeal may lead him, his heart will never be satisfied, because he knows that his zeal is but based on speculation and reasoning. He will never be sure whether his practice is God-pleasing. He is also aware that there are among the gentiles some who are even more zealous than he. Now I wish to ask thee concerning the Erub, which is one of the licences of the law of Sabbath. How can we make lawful a thing which God has forbidden by means so paltry and artificial.

51. The Rebbi: Heaven forbid that all those pious men and Sages should concur in untying one of the knots of the divine law. Their intention was to make it tighter and therefore they said: Build a fence round the law. Part of this is the Rebbinic prohibition of carrying things out of private to public ground or vice versa, a prohibition not of Mosaic origin. In constructing this fence, they introduced this licence, to prevent their religious zeal ranking with the Torah, and at the same time to give people some liberty in moving about. This liberty was gained in a perfectly lawful way and takes the form of the Erub, which marks a line between what is entirely legal, the fence itself, and the secluded part inside the latter.

52. Al Khazari: This is enough for me. Yet I cannot believe that an Erub is strong enough to restore a connexion between two areas.

53. The Rebbi: In this case the whole law is inefficient in thy opinion. Dost, thou consider the release of money, property, persons, and slaves valid by assuring the right of property or last will? Likewise, the divorce of a woman, or a second marriage, after having been single, by means of the formula: Write, sign and hand her the letter of divorce; or her singleness after having been married? All these matters depend upon a ceremony or a formula and are laid down in the Third Book of Moshe. The leprosy of a garment or house officially depends upon the declaration of **clean** or **unclean** by a priest. The holy character of the Tabernacle was subject to its being erected by Moshe and anointed with the anointing oil. The consecration of the priests depended upon the initiatory sacrifices and wave offerings; that of the Levites upon purifying and wave offerings.

Unclean persons were purified by means of 'water of separation. to which were added ashes of the red heifer, hyssop, and scarlet. The redemption of a house required two birds. All these ceremonies, the remission of sins on the Day of Atonement, the cleansing of the sanctuary from impurities by means of the he-goat of Azazel, with all accompanying ceremonies; the blessing of Israel through Aaron's uplifted hands and the reciting of the verse: the Lord bless thee; upon every one of these ceremonies the Divine Influence rested. Religious ceremonies are, like the work of nature, entirely determined by God, but beyond the power of man. Formations of nature, are, as thou canst see, composed of accurately measured proportions of the four elements. A trifle renders them perfect and gives them their proper animal or plant form. Every mixture receives the shape beseeming it, but can also lose it through a trifle. The egg may be spoiled by the slight accident of too much heat or cold, or a movement, and become unable to receive the form of a chicken which otherwise the hen achieves by sitting on it three weeks. Who, then, can weigh actions upon which the Divine Influence rest, save God alone? This is the error committed by alchymists and necromancers. The former thought, indeed, that they could weigh the elementary fire on their scales, and produce what they wished, and thus alter the nature of materials, as is done in living beings by natural heat which transforms food into blood, flesh, bone and other organs. They toil to discover a fire of the same kind, but are misled by accidental results of their experiments, not based on calculation, just in the same manner as the discovery was made that from the planting of seed within the womb man arises. When those necromancers heard that the appearance of the Divinity from Adam down to the children of Israel was gained by sacrifices, they thought it was the result of meditation and research; that the prophets were but deeply learned persons who accomplished these wonders by means of calculation. Then they, on their part, were anxious to fix sacrifices to be offered up at certain times and astrological opportunities, accompanied by ceremonies and burning of incense which their calculations prescribed. They even composed astrological books and other matters the mention of which is forbidden. Beside these, the adepts of magic formulas, having heard that a prophet had been spoken to in this or that manner, or had experienced a miracle, imagined that the words were the cause of the miracle. They, therefore endeavoured to accomplish a similar feat. The artificial is not like the natural. Religious deeds are, however, like nature. Being ignorant of their designs one thinks it but play till the results becomes apparent. Then one praises their guide and mover, and professes belief in him. Suppose thou hast heard nothing of cohabitation and its consequences, but thou feelest thyself attracted by the lowest of female organs. If thou considerest the degradation of a woman's surrender, or the ignominy of surrendering to a woman, thou wouldst say wonderingly: this is as vain as it is absurd. But when thou seest a being like thyself born of a woman, then dost thou marvel and notice that thou art one of the preservers of mankind created by God to inhabit the earth. It is the same with religious actions fixed by God. Thou slaughterest a lamb and smearest thyself with its blood, in skinning it, cleaning its entrails, washing, dismembering it and sprinking its blood. Then thou arrangest the wood, kindlest the fire, placing the body on it. If this were not done in consequence of a divine command, thou wouldst think little of all these actions and believe that they estrange thee from God rather than bring thee near to Him. But as soon as the whole is properly accomplished, and thou seest the divine fire, or dost notice in thyself a new spirit, unknown before, or seest true visions and great apparitions, thou art aware that this is the fruit of the preceding actions, as well as of the great influence with which thou hast come in contact. When arrived at this goal care not that thou must die. Thy death is but the decay of thy body, whilst the soul having reached this step, cannot descend from it nor be removed. This will shew thee that the approach to God is only possible through the medium of God's command, and there is no road to the knowledge of the commands of God except by way of prophesy, but not by means of speculation and reasoning. There is, however, no other connexion between us and these commands except truthful tradition. Those who have handed down these laws to us were not a few sporadic individuals, but a multitude of learned and lofty men nearly approaching the prophets. And if the bearers of the Law had only been the priests, Levites and the Seventy Elders, the chain beginning with Moshe himself would never have been interrupted.

54. Al Khazari: I only know that the people of the second Temple forgot the Torah, and were ignorant of the law of Succah till they found it written. A similar thing happened with the law that an Ammonite shall not enter the congregation of God. With regard to these two points, it is said: They found written. This proves that they had lost the knowledge of the law.

55. The Rebbi: If this be so we are to-day more learned and erudite than they, since we think we know the Torah.

56. Al Khazari: That is what I say.

57. The Rebbi: Should we be commanded to

bring a sacrifice, would we know how and where to slaughter it, catch its blood, skin and dismember it, and into how many pieces, how to offer it up, how to sprinkle the blood, what to do with its meal and wine offering; with what songs to accompany it; what duties of holiness, purity, anointment, clothing, and demeanour the priests had to observe; how, when and where they should eat the holy meat, and other matters which it would lead us too far to commemorate.

58. Al Khazari: We cannot know this without a priest or prophet.

59. The Rebbi: See how the people of the second Temple were engaged many years in the construction of the altar, till God assisted them to build the Temple and the walls. Dost, thou think that they brought offerings in a haphazard fashion.

60. Al Khazari: A burnt offering cannot be an offering made by fire a sweet savour being a law not dependent on reasoning-except if all its details are arranged on the authority and command of God. The people were also well acquainted with the regulations of the Day of Atonement, which are more important than the regulations of the Succah. All these things required the detailed instruction of a teacher.

61. The Rebbi: Should a person versed in these minute regulations of the Torah have been ignorant of the way how to construct a hut, or of the law concerning the Ammonites.

62. Al Khazari: What can I say, then, about 'they found written.

63. The Rebbi: The compiler of the Holy Writ did not pay so much attention to hidden matters as to those generally known. He, therefore, mentions nothing of the wisdom Yehoshua had received from God and from Moshe, but only the days when he stood at the Jordan, the day when the sun stood still, and the day of the circumcision, since these matters concerned the whole people. The tales of Samson, Deborah, Gideon, Samuel, David and Shlomo contain nothing about their own learning and religious practices. In the history of Shlomo we find an account of his luxurious table, great wealth, but of his great wisdom nothing except the case of the two women, because this took place in public. The wisdom he displayed in his intercourse with the Queen of Sheba and elsewhere is not mentioned, because it was not the author's intention to relate anything that did not concern or interest the whole people. Special records referring to special individuals only, are lost with the exception of a few, besides the magnificent prophetic speeches which everyone took a delight in learning by heart on account of their lofty contents and noble language. Even of the history of Ezra and Nehemiah nothing is related except that which concerned the whole people. The day of the building of the tabernacles was a public affair, because on that day the people set out to ascend the mountains and gather olive, myrtle and palm branches. The words: they found written, mean that the whole people gave attention to them and commenced to build their tabernacles. The erudite were not unacquainted with the details of the law, and still less with the general tenor of it. The author's intention was to single out this day, as well as the other one on which the Ammonite and Moabite wives were divorced. This was a remarkable day, when men had to divorce their wives and the mothers of their children, a grave and painful matter. I do not believe that any other people than the chosen would give a similar proof of their obedience to their Lord. It is on account of this public affair that the words: they found written, were said. It means that, when the public Reader read the words: An Ammonite or Moabite shall not enter... the people was moved, and a great perturbation arose on that day.

64. Al Khazari: Give me an example of the manner of tradition which proves its verity.

65. The Rebbi: Prophecy lasted about forty years during the second Temple among those elders who had the assistance of the Shekhinah from the first Temple. Individually acquired prophecy had ceased with the removal of the Shekhinah, and only appeared in extraordinary times or on account of great force, as that of Abraham, Moshe, the expected MASHIACH, Eliyahu and their equals. In them the Shekhinah found a worthy abode, and their very existence helped their contemporaries to gain the degree. of prophecy. The people, after their return, still had Haggai, Zechariah, Ezra and others. Forty years later these prophets were succeeded by an assembly of Sages, called the Men of the Great Synode. They were too numerous to be counted. They had returned with Zerubbabel and inherited their tradition from the Prophets, as it is said: The prophets **Handed** [the law] down to the Men of the Great Synode. The next generation was that of the High Priest Simon the Just and his disciples and friends. He was followed by Antigonos of Socho of great fame. His disciples were Ṣadok and Boethos who were the originators of the sects called after them Saddocaeans and Boethosians. The next was Yose ben Joezer the most pious among the priests, and Yosef ben Johanan and their friends. With regard to the former it was said: At the death of Yose ben Joezer the grapes ceased, as it is said: No grapes to eat; For no sin of his was know from

Kuzari — Third Essay

his youth to his death. He was followed by Yehoshua ben Peraḥyah whose history is known. Among his disciples was **Ysu** the Nazarene, and Nittai of Arbela was his contemporary. After him came Yehuda ben Tabbai and Simon ben Shetaḥ, with the friends of both. At this period arose the doctrine of the Karaites in consequence of an incident between the Sages and King Yannai who was a priest. His mother was under suspicion of being a **profane** woman. One of the Sages alluded to this, saying to him: Be satisfied, O king Yannai, with the royal crown, but leave the priestly crown to the seed of Aaron. His friends prejudiced him against the Sages, advising him to browbeat, expel, and scatter or kill them. He replied: If I destroy the Sages what will become of our Law. There is the written law, they replied, whoever wishes to study it may come and do so; take no heed of the oral law. He followed their advice and expelled the Sages and among them Simon ben Shetaḥ, his son-in-law. Rabbanism was laid low for some time. The other party tried to establish a law built on their own conception, but failed, till Rebbi Simon ben Shetaḥ returned with his disciples from Alexandria, and restored tradition to its former condition. Karaism had, however, taken root among people who rejected the oral law, and called all kinds of proofs to their aid, as we see to-day. As regards the Sadocaeans and Boethosians, they are the sectarians who are anathemised in our prayer. The followers of Jesus are the Baptists who adopted the doctrine of baptism, being baptized in the Jordan. The Karaites turned their attention to the fundamental principles, deducing the special laws from them by means of arguments. The damage often extended to the roots, through their ignorance rather than intention. The next generation was that of Shemayah and Abtalion, whose disciples were Hillel and Shammai. Hillel was famous for his learning and gentleness. He was a descendant of David and lived a hundred and twenty years. He had thousands of pupils. The following was said about the most select of these: Hillel the elder had eighty disciples. Thirty were worthy of association with the Shekhinah; thirty were fit to declare embolismic years, and twenty stood between the two former groups. The greatest of them was Yehonaton ben Uzziel, the least of them was Rabban Yehonaton ben Zakkai, who left unstudied no verse in the Torah, nor Mishnah, Talmud, Halakha, Agada, explanatory rules of the Sages and Scribes, nor any word of the law code. It was said concerning him, that he never held a profane conversation, was always the last and first in the house of study, never slept there even for a few minutes, never walked four yards without a word of Torah or phylacteries, never sat idle, but studied deeply. No one lectured to his pupils but he, said nothing but what he had heard from the mouth of his teacher, and never said that it was time to leave the house of study. This was also characteristic of his disciple Rebbi Eliezer. Rabban Yehonaton ben Zakkai lived a hundred and twenty years like his master, and saw the second Temple. Among his disciples was Rebbi Eliezer ben Hyrcanos, the author of the Chapters of Rebbi Eliezer, a famous work on astronomy, calculation of the spheres and earth and other profound astronomical subjects. His pupil was Rebbi Ishmael ben Elisha, the High Priest. He is the author of the works entitled Hekhaloth, Hakharath Panim, and the Ma'ase Merkabah, because he was initiated in the secrets of this science, being worthy of a degree near prophecy. He is responsible for the following utterance: Once I entered the Holy of Holiest in order to burn the incense, and I saw Akhteriel Yah, the Lord of Hosts, etc. Another pupil of his was the famous Rebbi Yehoshua between whom and Rabban Gamaliel occurred the well-known affair; further Rebbi Yose, and Rebbi Elazar ben Arakh. Of the last named it was said: If all Sages of Israel were placed on one scale and Elazar ben Arakh on the other, he would outweigh them, beside those famous men and many Sages, priests and Levites whose calling was the study of the law, there flourished undisturbed in the same period the seventy learned members of the Synhedrion on whose authority officials were appointed or

Kuzari — Third Essay

deposed. With reference to this it is told: Rebbi Simon ben Yoḥai said: I heard from the mouth of the seventy elders on the day when Rebbi Eliezer ben Azariah was appointed President of the Academy. These seventy had a hundred followers, the latter -thousands; for, seventy such accomplished men can best be selected from hundreds standing beneath them and so on by degrees. In the next generation after the destruction of the Temple, there lived Rebbi Akibah and Rebbi Tarfon and Rebbi Jose of Galilee with their friends. Rebbi Akibah reached a degree so near prophecy that he held intercourse with the spiritual world, as it is said: Four persons entered paradise; one of them peeped in and died, the other did the same and was hurt; the third did likewise and cut the plants down, and only one entered in peace and left in peace. This was Rebbi Akabah. The one who died was unable to bear the glance of the higher world, and his body collapsed. The second lost his mind and whispered divine frenzy without benefiting mankind. The third fell into bad ways, because he ascended above human intelligence and said: Human actions are but instruments which lead up to spiritual heights. Having reached these, I care not for religious ceremonies. He was corrupt and corrupted others, erred and caused others to err. Rebbi Akibah conversed with both worlds without harm, and it was said of him: He was as worthy of associating with the

Shekhinah as Moshe, but the period was not propitious. He was one of the ten martyrs, and during his torture enquired of his pupils, whether the time of reading the Shema had arrived. They answered: O our master; even now? All my days, he answered, I endeavoured to practise the words: "with all thy heart and all thy soul-even if it costs thee thy life"; now, when the opportunity has arisen, I will make them true. He protracted the eḥad till his soul fled.

66. Al Khazari: In this way one may spend a happy life, and die a happy, death, and then live an eternal life in never-ceasing bliss.

67. The Rebbi: In the next generation lived Rebbi Meir, Rebbi Yehuda, Rebbi Simon ben Azzai, and Rebbi Ḥananyah ben Teradion and their friends. They were followed by Rebbi, viz. Rebbi Yehuda Hannasi, our teacher. His contemporaries were Rebbi Nathan, Rebbi Yehoshua ben Korḥah, and many others who were the last teachers of the Mishnah, also called Tannaim. They were followed by the Amoraim, who are the authorities of the Talmud. The Mishnah was compiled in the year 530, according the era of the **Documents**, which corresponds to the year 150 after the destruction of the Temple, and 530 years after the termination of prophecy. In the Mishnah were reproduced those sayings and doings

Kuzari — Third Essay

which-few out of many-we have quoted. They treated the Mishnah with the same care as the Torah, arranging it in sections, chapters and paragraphs. Its traditions are so reliable that no suspicion of invention could be upheld. Besides this the Mishnah contains a large amount of pure Hebrew which is not borrowed from the Torah. It is greatly distinguished by terseness of language, beauty of style, excellence of composition, and the comprehensive employment of homonyms, applied in a lucid way, leaving neither doubt nor obscurity. This is so striking that every one who looks at it with genuine scrutiny must be aware that mortal man is incapable of composing such a work without divine assistance. Only he who is hostile to it, who does not know it, and never endeavoured to read and study it, hearing some general and allegorical utterances of the Sages deems them senseless and defective, just as one who judges a person after meeting him, without having conversed with him for any length of time. The following saying of Rebbi Nahum the Scribe will show how the Sages based their learning on that of the prophets: I have heard from Rebbi Mayyasha, who learnt from the **pairs**, who had it from the prophets as an ordination given to Moshe from Sinai.' They were careful not to hand down the teachings of single individuals, as is shown by the following saying uttered on the deathbed of one of them, to his son: 'My son, retract thy opinion on four subjects which I have taught thee. Wherefore, asked the son, 'didst thou not retract thine. I learnt, answered the father, 'from many who, in their turn, had learnt from many. I kept to my tradition, and they to theirs. Thou, however, didst learn only from one person. It is better to neglect the teachings of a single individual, and to accept that of the majority. These are a few sayings, like a drop from the sea, showing the excellence of the traditions of the Mishnah. To give thee a sketch of the traditions and traditionists of the Talmud, and its methods, sentences and aphorisms, would lead us too far. And if there is in it many a thing which is considered less attractive to-day, it was yet held proper in those days.

68. Al Khazari: Indeed, several details in their sayings appear to me inferior to their general principles. They employ verses of the Torah in a manner without regard to common sense. One can only say that the application of such verses once for legal deductions, another time for homiletic purposes, does not tally with their real meaning. Their Agadas and tales are often against reason.

69. The Rebbi: Didst thou notice how strictly and minutely the comments on the Mishnah and Boraitha are given? They speak with a thoroughness and lucidity which do equal justice both to the words and meaning of them.

70. Al Khazari: I am well aware to what perfection they brought the art of dialectics, but this is an argument which cannot be refuted.

71. The Rebbi: May we assume that he who proceeds with so much thoroughness should not know as much of the contents of a verse as we know.

72. Al Khazari: This is most unlikely. Two cases are possible. Either we are ignorant of their method of interpreting the Torah, or the interpreters of the Rebbinic law are not identical with those of the Holy Writ. The latter point of view is absurd. It is seldom that we see them give a verse a rational and literal rendition, but, on the other hand, we never find them interpret a halakha except on the lines of strict logic.

73. The Rebbi: Let us rather assume two other possibilities. Either they employ secret methods of interpretation which we are unable to discern, and which were handed down to them, together with the method of the Thirteen Rules of Interpretation, or they use Biblical verses as a kind of fulcrum of interpretation in a method called Asmakhta, and make them a sort of hall mark of tradition. An instance is given in the following verse: And the Lord God commanded the man, saying, of every tree of the garden thou mayest freely eat. It forms the basis of the **seven Noahide laws** in the following manner: He commanded refers to jurisdiction. The Lord refers to prohibition of blasphemy. God refers to prohibition of idolatry. The man refers to prohibition of murder. Saying refers to prohibition of incest. Of every tree of the garden, prohibition of rape. Thou mayest surely eat, a prohibition of flesh from the living animal. There is a wide difference between these injunctions and the verse. The people, however, accepted these seven laws as tradition, connecting them with the verse as aid to memory. It is also possible that they applied both methods of interpreting verses, or others which are now lost to us. Considering the well-known wisdom, piety, zeal, and number of the Sages which excludes a common plan, it is our duty to follow them. If we feel any doubt, it is not due to their words, but to our own intelligence. This also applies to the Torah and its contents. We must ascribe the defective understanding of it to ourselves. As to the Agadas, many serve as basis and introduction for explanations and inunctions. For instance: the saying, When the Lord descended to Egypt, etc. is designed to confirm the belief that the delivery from Egypt was a deliberate act of God, and not an accident, nor achieved with the assistance of human plotting, spirits, stars, and angels, jinn, or any other fanciful creation of the mind. It was done by God's providence alone. Statements of this kind are introduced by the word kibejakhol, which means: If this could be so and so, it would be so and so. Although this is not to be found in the Talmud, but only in a few other works, it is to be so understood wherever it is found. This is also the meaning of the words of Micaiah, when he said to Ahab: I saw the Lord sitting on his throne... host of heaven. And the Lord said, who shall persuade Ahab.... And there came forth a spirit, etc. As a matter of fact all that he intended conveying was: Behold, the Lord has put a lying spirit in the mouth of all these prophets. Verses of this kind serve as a fulcrum and induction, rendering a subject eloquent, apposite, and showing that it is based on truth. To the same category belong tales of visions of spirits, a matter which is not strange in such pious men. Some of the visions they saw were the consequence of their lofty thoughts and pure minds, others were really apparent, as was the case with those seen by the prophets. Such is the nature of the **Bath Qol** [Voice from Heaven], often heard during the time of the second Temple, and regarded as ranking next to prophecy and the Divine voice. Do not consider strange what Rebbi Ishmael said: I heard a voice cooing like a dove, etc. For the histories of Moshe and Eliyahu prove that such a thing is possible, and when a true account is given, it must be accepted as such. In a similar sense we must take the words: 'Woe unto me that I have destroyed my house, which is of the same character as: And it repented the Lord... and it grieved Him at His heart. Other Rebbinic sayings are parables employed to express mysterious teachings which were not to be made public. For they are of no use to the masses, and were only handed over to a few select persons for research and investigation, if a proper person suitable-one in an age, or in several-could be found. Other sayings appear senseless on the face of them, but that they have their meaning, becomes apparent after but a little reflection. The following is an instance: Seven things were created prior to the world: Paradise, the Torah, the just, Israel, the throne of glory, Jerusalem, and the MASHIACH, the son of David. This is similar to the saying of some philosophers: The primary thought includes the final deed. It was the object of divine wisdom in the creation of the world to create the Torah, which was the essence of wisdom, and whose bearers are the just, among whom stands the throne of glory and the truly righteous, who are the most select, viz. Israel, and the proper place for them was Jerusalem, and only the best of men, viz. the MASHIACH, son of David, could be associated with them, and they all entered Paradise. Figuratively speaking, one must assume that they were created prior to the world. Seemingly against

Kuzari — Third Essay

common sense is also the saying: Ten things were created in the twilight, viz. the opening of the earth, the opening of the spring, the mouth of the she ass, etc., as otherwise the Torah were out of harmony with nature. Nature claims to pursue its regular course, whilst the Torah claims to alter this regular course. The solution is that ordinary natural phenomena are altered within natural limits, since they had been primarily fixed by the divine will, and clearly laid down from the six days of creation. I will not deny, O King of the Khazars, that there are matters in the Talmud of which I am unable to give thee a satisfactory explanation, nor even bring them in connexion with the whole. These things stand in the Talmud through the conscientiousness of the disciples, who followed the principle that 'even the commonplace talk of the Sages requires study. They took care to reproduce only that which they had heard from their teachers, striving at the same time to understand everything they had heard from their masters. In this they went so far as to render it in the same words, although they may not have grasped its meaning. In this case they said: Thus, have we been taught and have heard. Occasionally the teacher concealed from his pupils the reasons which prompted him to make certain statements. But the matter came down to us in this form, and we think little of it, because we do not know its purport. For the whole of this relates to topics which do not touch on lawful or unlawful matters. Let us not therefore trouble about it, and the book will lose nothing if we consider the points discussed here.

74. Al Khazari: Thou hast pleased me greatly, and strengthened my belief in tradition. Now I should like to learn something of the scientific pursuits of the Sages. But previously give me a discourse on the names of God. On this subject thou canst speak at greater length.

Fourth Essay

1. THE Rebbi: ELOHIM is a term signifying the ruler, or governor of the world, if I allude to the possession of the whole of it, and of a portion, if I refer to the powers either of nature or the spheres, or of a human judge. The word has a plural form, because it was so used by gentile idolators, who believed that every deity was invested with astral and other powers. Each of these was called Eloah; their united forces were therefore, called Elohim. They swore by them, and behaved as if bound to abide by their judgments. These deities were as numerous as are the forces which sway the human body and the universe. 'Force' is a name for any of the causes of motion. Every motion arises from a force of its own, to the exclusion of other forces. The spheres of the sun and moon are not subject to one force, but to different ones. These people did not take into account the prime power from which all these forces emanated, because they did not acknowledge its existence. They asserted that the sum total of these forces was styled Eloah, just as the sum total of the forces which control the human body was called 'soul.' Or they admitted the existence of God, but maintained that to serve Him was of no use. They considered Him too far removed and exalted to have any knowledge of us, much less to care about us. Far from God are such notions. As a result of their theories they worshipped, not one being, but many, which they styled 'Elohim.' This is a collective form which comprises all causes equally. A more exact and more-lofty name is to be found in the form known as the Tetragrammaton. This is a proper noun, which can only be indicated by attributes, but has no location, and was formerly unknown. If He was commonly styled 'Elohim,' the Tetragrammaton was used as special name. This is as if one asked: Which God is to be worshipped, the sun, the moon, the heaven, the signs of the zodiac, any star, fire, a spirit, or celestial angels, etc.; each of these, taken singly, has an activity and force, and causes growth and decay? The answer to this question is: **The Lord**, just as if one would say: So, and So, or a proper name, as Ruben or Simeon, supposing that these names indicate their personalities.

2. Al Khazari: How can I individualise a being, if I am not able to point to it, and can only prove its existence by its actions.

3. The Rebbi: It can be designated by prophetic or visionary means. Demonstration can lead astray. Demonstration was the mother of heresy and destructive ideas. What was it, if not the wish to demonstrate, that led the dualists to assume two eternal causes? And what led materialists to teach that the sphere was not only eternal, but its own primary cause, as well as that of other matter? The worshippers of fire and sun are but the result of the desire to demonstrate. There are differences in the ways of demonstration, of which some are more extended than others. Those who go to the utmost length are the philosophers, and the ways of their arguments led them to teach of a Supreme Being which neither benefits nor injures, and knows nothing of our prayers, offerings, obedience, or disobedience, and that the world is as eternal as He himself. None of them applies a distinct proper name to God, except he who hears His address, command, or prohibition, approval for obedience, and reproof for disobedience. He bestows on Him some name as a designation for Him who spoke to him, and he is convinced that He is the Creator of the world from nought. The first man would never have known Him if He had not addressed, rewarded and punished him, and had not created Eve from one of his ribs. This gave him the conviction that this was the Creator of the world, whom he designated by words and attributes, and styled **Lord**. Without this he would have been satisfied with the name Elohim, neither perceiving what He was, nor whether He was a unity or many, whether He was cognizant of individuals or not. Cain and Abel were made acquainted with the nature of His being by the communications of their father as well as by prophetic intuition. Then Noah, Abraham, Itzhak and Yaakov, Moshe and the prophets called Him intuitively 'Lord,' as also did the people, having been taught by tradition that His influence and guidance were with men. His influence also being with the pious, they comprehended Him by means of intermediaries called: glory, Shekhinah, dominion, fire, cloud, likeness, form, the appearance of the bow, etc. For they proved to them that He had spoken to them, and they styled it: Glory of God. Occasionally they addressed the holy ark by the name of God, as it is written: Rise up, O Lord, when they made a start, and 'Return, O Lord' when they halted, or 'God is gone up with a shout, the Lord with the sound of the trumpet', With all this only the ark of the Lord is meant. Sometimes the name **Lord** was applied to the connecting link between God and Israel, as it is written: Do not I hate them, O Lord, that hate thee. By 'haters of the Lord' are meant those who hate the name, or covenant, or the law of God. For there exists no connexion between God and any other nation, as He pours out His light only on the select people. They are accepted by Him, and He by them. He is called 'the God of Israel,' whilst they are 'the people of the Lord,' and 'the people of the God of Abraham.' Even supposing some nations had followed Him and worshipped Him, their conversion being the result of hearsay and tradition, yet where do we find His acceptance of them and His connexion with them, His pleasure in their obedience, His anger for their disobedience? We see them left to nature and chance by which their prosperity or misfortune are determined, but not by an influence which proves to be of divine origin alone. Thus, also we alone are meant in the words: 'So the Lord alone did lead him, and there was no strange god with him. The Tetragrammaton is a name exclusively employable by us, as no other people knows its true meaning. It is a proper name which takes no article, as is the case with Elohim in the form haelohim. It belongs, therefore, to the prerogatives by which we are distinguished. Although its meaning is hidden, the letters of which it is composed speak. For it is the letters alef, he, wav and yod which cause all consonants to be sounded, as no letter can be pronounced as long as it is not supported by one of these four, viz. a by alef, and he, u by wav, and i by yod. They form, so to speak, the spirit in the bodies of the consonants. The name Oh is like the Tetragrammaton. As to EH'YEH, it can be derived from the latter name, or from the root hayah, and its tendency is to prevent the human mind from pondering over an incomprehensible but real entity. When Moshe asked: 'And they shall say to me, what is His name?' the answer was: Why should they ask concerning things they are unable to grasp? In a like manner the angel answered: 'Why askest

Kuzari — Fourth Essay

thou thus after my name, seeing it is secret. Say to them eh'yeh, which means: 'I am that I am,' the existing one, existing for you whenever you seek me. Let them search for no stronger proof than My presence among them, and name Me accordingly. Moshe therefore answered: Eh'yeh has sent me to you. God had previously given a similar proof to Moshe in the words: Certainly, I will be with thee, and this shall be a token unto thee, etc. viz. that I have sent thee, and am with thee everywhere. This is followed by a similar phrase, viz. The God of your fathers, the God of Abraham, the God of Itzhak and the God of Yaakov, persons known to have been favoured by the Divine Influence perpetually. As regards the terms: Elohe haelohim, it is a designation for the fact that all creative forces are depending upon God, who arranges and guides them. **Lord of lords** has the same meaning. **EL** is derived from ayaluth, being the source of the forces [of nature], but exalted above them. The expression: Who is like unto thee among the elim, is, therefore, permissible, placing el into the plural form. HOLY expresses the notion that He is high above any attribute of created beings, although many of these are applied to him metaphorically. For this reason, Isaiah heard an endless: 'Holy, holy, holy,' which meant that God is too high, too exalted, too holy, and too pure for any impurity of the people in whose midst His light dwells to touch Him. For the same reason Isaiah saw him sitting upon a throne, high and lifted up. Holy is, further, a description of the spiritual, which never assumes a corporeal form, and which nothing concrete can possibly resemble. God is called: the Holy One of Israel, which is another expression for the Divine Influence connected with Israel himself and the whole of his posterity, to rule and guide them, but not to be merely in external contact with them. Not everyone who wishes is permitted to say, 'My God and Holy One!' except in a metaphorical and traditional way. In reality only a prophet or a pious person with whom the Divine Influence is connected may say so. For this reason, they said to the prophet: Pray to the Lord, thy God. The relation of this nation to others was to have been like that of a king to ordinary people, as it is written: Holy shall ye be, for holy am I the Lord, your God. **ADONAI**, spelt alef, daleth, nun, yod points to something which stands at such an immeasurable altitude that a real designation is impossible. Indication is possible in one direction only. We can point to things created by Him, and which form His immediate tools. Thus, we allude to the intellect, and say that its seat is in the heart or brain. We also say **this** or **that intellect**. In reality we can only point to a thing enclosed by a space. Although all organs obey the intellect, they do so through the medium of the heart or brain, which are its primary tools, which arc considered as the abode of the intellect. In a like manner we point to heaven, because it is employed to carry out the divine will directly, and without the assistance of intermediary factors. On the other hand, we cannot point to compound objects, because they can only operate with the assistance of intermediary causes, and are connected with God in a chain-like manner. For He is the cause of causes. He is also called - He who dwelleth in heaven, and 'For God is in heaven. One often says, Fear of heaven, and fearing heaven in secret, mercy shall come for them from heaven. In a similar way we speak of the pillar of fire, or the pillar of cloud, worship them, and say that God is therein, because this pillar carried out His will exclusively, unlike other clouds and fires which arise in the air from different causes. Thus, we also speak of the - devouring fire on the top of the mount, which the common people saw, as well as of the spiritual form which was visible only to the higher classes: under His feet as it were a paved work of a sapphire stone. He is further styled: Living God. The holy ark is alluded to as - The Lord of the whole earth, because miracles happened as long as it existed, and disappeared with it. We say that it is the eye which sees, whilst in reality it is the soul that sees. Prophets and pious Sages are spoken of in similar terms, because they, too, are original instruments of the divine will which employs them without meeting with unwillingness, and performs miracles through them. In illustration of this the Rebbis said: The words: Thou shalt fear the Lord thy God, include the learned disciples. He who occupies such a degree has a right to be styled - a man of God, a description comprising human and divine qualities, and as if one would say: godly man. Now in speaking of a divine being we use the appellation, Adonai-alef, daleth, nun, yod- as if we wished to say: O Lord. Metaphorically speaking, we point to a thing encompassed by a place as: 'He who dwells between the cherubim,' or 'He who dwells in Zion,' or, 'He who abides in Jerusalem.' The attributes of this kind are many, although His essence is only one. The variety arises from the variety of places where God's essence dwells, just as the rays of the sun are many whilst the sun is everywhere the same. This simile is not quite complete. Were only the rays of the sun visible, but not the sun itself, their origin would have to be demonstrated. I must enlarge on this subject a little more, because there are debatable points about it, viz. firstly, how it is possible to speak of space in connexion with a being that has no place; secondly, how can one believe that a subject to which one can point could be the Prime Cause? In reply to these objections, we say in the first instance, that the senses can only perceive the attributes of things, not the substrata themselves. In a prince e.g., thou perceivest his external and visible form and proportions. It is not these to which thou must render homage. Thou seest him in war in one habit, in his city in another, in his house in a third. Following thy judgment rather than thy perception, thou sayest that he is the king. He may appear first as a boy, then as a youth, then in his prime, and finally as an old man; or as a healthy or sick man, his appearance, manner, disposition and qualities being changed. Still thou considerest him to be the same and the king, because he has spoken to thee and given thee his commands. The royal side of him is but the intellectual and rational one, but this is essence, not limited to space and not to be pointed to, although thou dost so and sayest that he is the king. But if he is dead, and thou seest the same old form, thou wilt conclude that this is not the king, but a body which can be moved by whoso wishes, which depends upon chance and other peoples' humour, like a cloud in the air which one wind brings hither and other drives away, one wind gathers, another disperses. Previously he was a body which was subject to the royal will alone, resembling the divine pillar of cloud which no wind was able to disperse. Another instance is offered by the sun, which we see as a round, flat body, resembling a shield and giving forth light and heat, being in repose. Reason considers it to be a globe a hundred and sixty-six times larger than the globe of the earth, neither hot nor immovable, but moving in two opposite directions, from west to east, and from east to west, under conditions it would lead us too far to discuss. The senses have not the faculty of perceiving the essence of things. They only have the special power of perceiving the accidental peculiarities belonging to them which furnish reason with the arguments for their essence and causes. Why and wherefore are accessible to pure reason only. Everything that shares active intellect, like the angels, grasps the subjects in their true essence without requiring the medium of accessories. But our intellect which a priori is only theoretical, being sunk in matter, cannot penetrate to the true knowledge of things, except by the grace of God, by special faculties which He has placed in the senses, and which resemble those perceptible accessories, but are always found with the whole species. There is no difference between my perception and thine that this circumscribed disc, giving forth light and heat, is the sun. Should even these characteristics be denied by reason, this does no harm, because we can derive from it arguments for our purposes. Thus, also a sharp-eyed person, looking for a camel, can be assisted by a weak-eyed and squinting one who tells him that he has seen two cranes at a certain place. The sharp-eyed person then knows that the other has only seen a camel, and that the weakness of his eyes made him believe that it was a crane, and his squint that there were two cranes. In this way the sharp-eyed person can make use of the evidence of the weak-eyed one, whilst he excuses his faulty description by his defective sight. A similar relation prevails between senses and imagination on one side, and reason on the other. The Creator was as wise in arranging this relation between the exterior senses and the things perceived, as He was in fixing the relation between the abstract sense and the uncorporeal substratum. To the chosen among His creatures He has given an inner eye which sees things as they really are, without any alteration. Reason is thus in a position to come to a conclusion regarding the true spirit of these things. He to whom this eye has been given is clear-sighted indeed. Other people who appear to him as blind, he guides on their way. It is possible that this eye is the power of imagination as long as it is under the control of the intellect. It beholds, then, a grand and awful sight which reveals unmistakable truths. The best proof of its truth is the harmony prevailing among the whole of this species and those sights. By this I mean all the prophets. For they witnessed things which one described to the other in the same manner as we do with things we have seen. We testify to the sweetness of honey and the bitterness of the coloquinth. and if anyone contradicts us, we say that he has failed to grasp a fact of natural history. Those prophets without doubt saw the divine world with the inner eye; they beheld a sight which harmonized with their natural imagination. Whatever they wrote down, they endowed with attributes as if they had seen them in corporeal form. These attributes are true as far as regards what is sought by inspiration, imagination, and feeling; they are untrue as regards the reality which is sought by reason, as we have seen in the parable of the king. For anyone who says that he is a tall, white figure clothed in silk, and wearing the royal insignia on his head has spoken no untruth. Whilst he who says that this is none other than the intelligent, sagacious person, who issues commands and prohibitions, in this city, in this age, and rules this people, has not spoken an untruth either. If a prophet sees with his mind's eye the most perfect figure ever beheld in the shape of a king or judge, seated on his throne, issuing commands and prohibitions, appointing and deposing officials, then he knows that this figure resembles a powerful prince. But if he sees a figure bearing arms or writing utensils, or ready to undertake work, then he knows that this figure resembles an obedient servant. Do not find it out of place that man should be compared to God. Upon deeper consideration reason might compare him to light, because this is the noblest and finest of all material things, and which has the greatest power of encompassing the component parts of the world. If we reflect on the attributes, which are essential whether they be taken in metaphorical or real sense, such as: living, omniscient, almighty, omnipotent, guiding, arranging, giving everything its due, wise and just, we shall find nothing resembling God more closely than the rational soul-in other words, the perfect human being. But here we must lay stress on his human character, not on his corporeality, which he has in common with the plant, or on his being endowed with life which he has in common with the animals. Philosophers compared the world to a great man, and man to a small world. If this be so, God being the spirit, soul, intellect and life of the world-as He is called: the eternally Living, then rational comparison is plausible. Nay, a prophet's eye is more penetrating than speculation. His sight reaches up to the heavenly host direct, he sees the dwellers in heaven, and the spiritual beings which are near God, and others in human form. They are alluded to in the verse: Let us make man in our image after our likeness. The meaning is: I have displayed wisdom in arranging the creation in the following order: elements, metals, animals which live in the water as well as in the air, and those with fully developed senses and wonderful instincts. Next to this class there is only one which approaches the divine and celestial. God created man in the form of His angels and servants which are near Him, not in place but in rank, as we cannot speak of place in connexion with God. Even after these two comparisons, imagination can give him no other form than that of the noblest human being, who arranges order and harmony for the rest of mankind, in the same systematic way as God has done for the universe. At times the prophet sees princes deposed and others raised to the throne, and kingdoms judged, 'till the thrones were placed, and the Ancient of Days did sit; at other times he sees wrath poured out and the people in mourning on account of their threatened abandonment by Him, 'Who is sitting upon a throne high and lifted up... above it stood the seraphim. At other times, even outside the confines of prophecy, he sees the departure of the chariot as Ezekiel saw it, and retained it in his memory. For when the geographical limits of the land of prophecy were fixed, 'from the Red Sea, till the sea of the Philistines,' the desert of Sinai, Paran, Seir and Egypt were included. This area was also privileged. Whenever a person was found in it who fulfilled all the necessary conditions, these sights became distinctly visible to him, 'apparently, and not in dark speeches,' just as Moshe saw the Tabernacle, the sacrificial worship, and the land of Canaan in all its parts; or in the scene when, 'the Lord passed by before him.' Eliyahu had a vision also within this area. These things, which cannot be approached by speculation, have been rejected by Greek philosophers, because speculation negatives everything the like of which it has not seen. Prophets, however, confirm it, because they cannot deny what they were privileged to behold with their mind's eye. Such a number of them, living as they did in various epochs, could not have acted upon some common understanding. These statements were borne out by contemporary sages who had witnessed their prophetic afflatus. Had the Greek philosophers seen them when they prophesied and performed miracles, they would have acknowledged them, and sought by speculative means to discover how to achieve such things. Some of them did, so especially gentile philosophers. The name Adonai, [spelt alef, daleth, nun, yod] must be understood in a similar way, because of the idea of divine sovereignty which it conveys. We say: O my Lord, or, Messengership of the Lord, which is another name for divine ordination. Some angels are only created for the time being from fine elementary corpuscles, others are lasting, and are perhaps those spiritual beings of which the prophets speak. We have neither to refute nor to adopt their views. Concerning the visions seen by Isaiah, Ezekiel, and Daniel, there is some doubt whether their objects were newly created, or of the number of those lasting spiritual beings. **Glory of God** is that fine substance which follows the will of God, assuming any form God wishes to show to the prophet. This is one view. According to another view the Glory of

God means the whole of the angels and spiritual beings, as well as the throne, chariot, firmament, wheels, spheres, and other imperishable beings. All this is styled **Glory**, just as a king's retinue is called his splendour. Perhaps that was what Moshe desired, when he said: 'I beseech Thee, shew me Thy glory.' God fulfilled his wish on the condition that he should not see His face which no mortal could endure, as He said: And thou shalt see My back parts, but My face shall not be seen. This includes the glory which the prophet's eye could bear, and there are things in its wake which even our eye can behold, as the **cloud**, and the devouring fire, because we are accustomed to see them. The higher degrees of these are so transcendental that even prophets cannot perceive them. He, however, who boldly endeavours to do so impairs his constitution, even as the power of sight is impaired. People with weak eyes only see by subdued light after sunset, like the bat. Weak-eyed people can only see in the shadow, but people with strong eyes can see in sunlight. No eye, however, can look into the bright sun, and he who attempts to do so is stricken with blindness. Such is the explanation of the **Glory of God**, the Angels of the Lord, and the **Shekhinah of the Lord**, as they are called in the Torah. Occasionally they are applied to objects of nature, Full is the whole earth of His glory, or - His kingdom ruleth over all. In truth,

Kuzari — Fourth Essay

glory and kingdom do not become visible except to the pious, and the pure, and to the prophets who impart the conviction to the heretic that judgment and rule on earth belong to God, who knows every action of man. If this be so, it can truly be said, **The Lord is King**, and **The Glory of God shall be revealed**. The Lord shall reign for ever, thy God O Zion, unto all generations, say ye to Zion, thy God reigneth, the Glory of the Lord is risen upon thee. Now thou wilt not reject everything that has been said concerning such verses as: The similitude of the Lord shall he behold, they saw the Lord of Israel, nor ma'aseh merkabah and Sheur Komah, because in the opinion of some interpreters the reverence of God is implanted in the human mind, as it is written: That His fear may be before your faces.

4. Al Khazari: If there be conviction in the mind that God's is the kingdom, the unity, omnipotence, and omniscience, and that everything is dependent upon Him, He being dependent upon no one, then is not reverence and love for Him a necessary consequence, without such anthropomorphisms.

5. The Rebbi: This is a doctrine of philosophers. We see that the human soul shows fear whenever it meets with anything terrible, but not at the mere report of such a thing. It is likewise attracted by a beautiful form which strikes the eye, but not so much by one that is only spoken of. Do not believe him who considers himself wise in thinking that he is so far advanced that he is able to grasp all metaphysical problems with the abstract intellect alone, without the support of anything that can be conceived or seen, such as words, writing, or any visible or imaginary forms. Seest thou not that thou art not able even to collect the burden of thy prayer in thought alone, without reciting it? Neither canst thou reckon up to a hundred without speaking, still less if this hundred be composed of different numbers. Were it not for the sensible perception which encompasses the organization of the intellect by means of similar sayings, that organization could not be maintained. In this way, prophets images picture God's greatness, power, loving kindness, omniscience, life, eternity, government, and independence, the dependence of everything on Him, His unity, and holiness, and in one sudden flash stands revealed this grand and majestic figure with its splendour, its characteristics, the instruments which typify power, etc., the up-lifted hand, the unsheathed sword, fire, wind, thunder and lightning which obey his behest, the word which goes forth to warn, to announce what has happened, and to predict. Many angels stand humbly before Him, and He gives them according to their requirements without stint.

He raises the lowly, humbles the mighty, and holds out His hand to the repentant, saying to them: Who is conscious of a sin shall repent. He is wroth with the wicked, deposes and appoints, whilst before Him -thousand thousand minister unto Him. Such are the visions which the prophet sees in one second. Thus, fear and love come to him naturally, and remain in his heart for the whole of his life. He even yearns and longs to behold the vision again and again. Such a repetition was considered a great event for Shlomo, in the words: The Lord who has appeared to him twice. Will a philosopher ever achieve the same result.

6. Al Khazari: That is impossible. Thinking is like narrating, but one cannot recount two things at the same time. Should this even be possible, no one who hears them, can absorb them simultaneously. The details of a country and of its inhabitants which it is possible to see in one hour would not find room in a large volume, whilst in one moment love or hatred of a country could enter my heart. If all this were read to me from a book it would not impress me so greatly, but would, on the contrary, confuse my mind, being mixed up with errors, fancies and previous impressions. And nothing would be completely clear.

7. The Rebbi: We are like those weak-eyed

persons who cannot bear the brightness of the light. We, therefore, imitate the sharp-eyed who lived before us and were able to see. Now just as a person with sound eyes can only look at the sun, shew it to others and observe it from certain elevated spots, and at a certain hour of the day when it rises, so also, he who may gaze at the divine light, has his times and places in which he can behold it. These times are the hours of prayer, especially on days of repentance, and the places are those of prophecy.

8. Al Khazari: I see, then, that thou dost admit the dominion of hours, days, and places, as the astrologers do.

9. The Rebbi: We cannot deny that the heavenly spheres exercise influence on terrestrial matters. We must admit that the material components of growth and decay are dependent on the sphere, whilst the forms take their origin from Him who arranges and guides them, and makes them the instruments for the preservation of all the things which He wishes should exist. The particulars are unknown to us. The astrologer boasts of knowing them, but we repudiate it, and assert that no mortal can fathom them. If we find that any element of this science is based on the divine law, we accept it. But even then, we must rest satisfied with such astronomical proficiency as was possessed by the Sages, since we desire that it be supported by divine power, and correct withal. If this be wanting, it is but fiction, and there is more truth in our earthly lot than in the celestial one. He who is capable of gauging these matters is the real prophet; the place where they are visible is the true place of worship. For it is a divine place, and the law coming forth from it is the true religion.

10. Al Khazari: Certainly, if later religions admit the truth, and do not dispute it, then they all respect the place, and call it the stepping stone of the prophets, the gate of heaven, the place of gathering of the souls on the day of judgment. They, further, admit the existence of prophecy among Israel, whose forefathers were distinguished in a like manner. Finally, they believe in the work of creation, the flood, and nearly all that is contained in the Torah. They also perform pilgrimages to this hallowed place.

11. The Rebbi: I would compare them to proselytes who did not accept the whole law in all its branches, but only the fundamental principles, if their actions did not belie their words. Their veneration of the land of prophecy consists chiefly in words, and at the same time they also revere places sacred to idols. Such is the case in places in which an assembly happened to meet, but in which no sign of God became visible. Retaining the relics of ancient idolatry and feast days, they changed nothing but the forms. These were, indeed, demolished, but the relics were not removed. I might almost say that the verse in the Torah, occurring repeatedly: Thou shalt not serve strange gods, wood and stone. contains an allusion to those who worship the wood, and those who worship the stones We, through our sins, incline daily more towards them. It is true that they, like the people of Abimelech and Nineveh, believe in God, but they philosophize concerning God's ways. The leader of each of these parties maintained that he had found the divine light at its source, viz., in the Holy Land, and that there he ascended to heaven, and commanded that all the inhabitants of the globe should be guided in the right path. They turned their faces towards the land in prayer, but before long they changed and turned towards the place where the greatest number of their people lived. This is as if a person wished to guide all men to the place of the sun, because they are blind and do not know its course. He, however, leads them to the south or north pole, and tells them: "the sun is there, if you turn towards it, you will see it." But they see nothing. The first leader, Moshe, made the people stand by Mount Sinai, that they might see the light which he himself had seen, should they be able to see it in the same way. He, then, invited the Seventy Elders to see it, as it is written: 'They saw the God of Israel. Then he assembled the second convocation of Seventy Elders to whom he transferred so much of his prophetic spirit, that they equalled him, as is written: And he took of the spirit that was upon him and gave it unto the seventy elders. One related to the other concerning what they saw and heard. By these means all evil suspicion was removed from the people, lest they opined that prophecy was only the privilege of the few who claimed to possess it. For no common compact is possible among so many people, especially where large hosts of them are concerned, and equally well-informed as Elisha, who knew the day on which God would remove Eliyahu, as it is written: Knowest thou, that the Lord will take away thy master... to-day. Each elder served as a witness for Moshe, and admonished the people to keep the law.

12. Al Khazari: But the followers of other religions approach you more nearly than the philosophers.

13. The Rebbi: They are as far removed from us as the followers of a religion from a philosopher. The former seeks God not only for the sake of knowing Him, but also for other great benefits which they derive therefrom. The philosopher, however, only seeks Him that he may be able to describe Him accurately in detail, as he would describe the earth, explaining that it is in the centre of the great sphere, but not in that of the zodiac, etc. Ignorance of God would be no more injurious than would ignorance concerning the earth be injurious to those who consider it flat. The real benefit is to be found only in the cognizance of the true nature of things, in order to resemble the Active Intellect. Be he believer or freethinker, it does not concern him, if he is a philosopher. His axiom is that: God will do no good, neither will He do evil. If he believes in the eternity of matter, he cannot assume that there was a time when it did not exist prior to its creation. He opines that it was never non-existing, that it will never cease to exist, that God can only be called its creator in a metaphorical sense. The term **Creator**, and 'Maker' he explains as cause and prime mover of the world. Effect lasts as long as the cause does. If the latter is only potential, the former is potential; if real, real. God is cause in reality; that which is caused by Him remains, therefore, so long in existence as He remains its cause. We cannot blame philosophers for missing the mark, since they only arrived at this knowledge by way of speculation, and the result could not have been different, The most sincere among them speak to the followers of a revealed religion in the words of Socrates: My friends, I will not contest your theology, I say, however, that I cannot grasp it; I only understand human wisdom. These speculative religions are as far removed now as they were formerly near. If this were not so, Jeroboam and his party would be nearer to us, although they worshipped idols, as they were Israelites, inasmuch as they practised circumcision, observed the Sabbath, and other regulations, with few exceptions, which administrative emergencies had forced them to neglect. They acknowledged the God of Israel who delivered them from Egypt, in the same way as did the worshippers of the golden calf in the desert. The former class is at best superior to the latter inasmuch as they prohibited images. Since, however, they altered the **Kibla**, and sought Divine Influence where it is not to be found, altering at the same time the majority of ceremonial laws, they wandered far from the straight path.

14. Al Khazari: A wide difference should be made between the party of Jeroboam and that of Ahab. Those who worship Baal are idolators in every respect. In reference to this Eliyahu said: If the Lord be God, follow Him; but if Baal, follow him. For this reason, the Sages are in a dilemma as to how Josaphat could partake of Ahab's food. They have no such doubts concerning Jeroboam. Eliyahu's protest had no reference to the worship of the calves, since he said: I have been very jealous for the Lord, the God of Israel. The party of Jeroboam considered itself belonging to the Lord, the

God of Israel,' also all their actions, their prophets were the prophets of God, whilst the prophets of Ahab were Baal's prophets. God appointed Jehu to destroy the works of Ahab. He proceeded with much zeal and cunning, saying: Ahab served Baal a little, Jehu will serve him much. He destroyed all vestiges of Baal, indeed, but did not touch the calves. The worshippers of the first calf, the party of Jeroboam, and the worshippers of the heights and the image of Micah had no other idea than that they were serving the God of Israel, though in the way they did it they were disobedient and deserved death. This is as if a man marries his sister either under compulsion or from lust, and yet observes the marriage regulations as commanded by God. Or if one would eat swine's flesh, but carefully observe the rules concerning slaughtering, blood and ritual.

15. The Rebbi: Thou hast called attention to a debatable point, although there is no doubt about it for me. But we have wandered from our subject, viz. the attributes. To return to it, let me explain the matter to thee by a simile taken from the sun. The sun is only a single body, whilst those receiving their light from it are in many ways dependent on each other. The most fitted to annex its lustre are the ruby, crystal, pure air and water, and their light is therefore called transparent. On glittering stones and polished surfaces, it is called luminous; on wood, earth, etc., visible light, and on all other things it is simply designated light without any specific qualification. This general term, light, corresponds to what we call Elohim, as is now clear. Transparent light corresponds to **Eternal**, a proper name which describes especially the relation between Him and His earthly creatures, I mean, the prophets, whose souls are refined and susceptible to His light, which penetrates them, just as the sunlight penetrates the crystal and ruby. Their souls take their origin and development as has been explained before from Adam. Essence and heart of Adam reappear in every generation and age, whilst the large mass of mankind is set aside as husks, leaves, mud, etc. The God of this essence is only and solely Adonai, and because He established a connexion with man, the name Elohim was altered after the creation into Adonai Elohim. This the Sages express in the words: A 'full name over a full universe. The world was but completed with the creation of man who forms the heart of all that was created before him. No intelligent person will misunderstand the meaning conveyed by **Elohim**, although this is possible with regard to Adonai, because prophecy is strange and rare in single individuals, and much more so in a multitude. For this reason, Pharaoh disbelieved and said: I know not the Lord, as if he interpreted the Tetragrammaton in the way penetrating light is understood, and was

Kuzari — Fourth Essay

reminded by it of God whose light is intimately attached to man. Moshe supplemented his words by adding: the God of the Hebrews, in order to call to mind the patriarchs who testified by means of prophecy and marvels. Elohim was a name well known in Egypt. The first Pharaoh said to Yosef: Forasmuch as Elohim has shewn thee all this, and A man in whom the spirit of Elohim is. This is as if one man alone sees the sun, knows the points of its rising and course, whilst we others never behold it and live-in shadow and mist. We find, then, that his house has much lighter than ours, because he is acquainted with the course of the sun and can arrange his windows according to his desire. We also see his crops and plantations thriving, which, as he says, is the consequence of his knowing the course of the sun. We however, would deny this, and ask: What is the sun? We know the light and its manifold advantages, but it comes to us merely by accident. To me, he would answer, it comes as much and as frequently as I desire, because I know its cause and course. If I am prepared for it and arrange all my plans and works for their proper seasons, I reap the full benefit of it. A substitute for Adonai is Presence, as in the verse: My Presence shall go with thee, or - If thy Presence go not with me. The same is meant in the verse: Let my Lord, I pray Thee, go among us. The meaning of Elohim can be grasped by way of speculation, because a

Kuzari — Fourth Essay

Guide and Manager of the world is a postulate of Reason. Opinions differ on the basis of different speculations, but that of the philosophers is the best on the subject. The meaning of Adonai, however, cannot be grasped by speculation, but only by that intuition and prophetic vision which separates man, so to speak, from his kind, and brings him in contact with angelic beings, imbuing him with a new spirit, as it is written: Thou shalt be turned into another man, God gave him another heart, A spirit came over Amasai. The hand of the Lord was upon me. Uphold me with Thy free spirit. All these circumscribe the Holy Spirit which enwraps the prophet in the hour of his ministry, the Nazirite, and the MASHIACH, when they are anointed for priesthood, or for the royal dignity by a prophet; or when God aids and strengthens him in any matter; or when the priest makes prophetic utterances by means of the mystic power derived from the use of the **Urim and Tummim**. Then all previous doubts concerning Elohim are removed, and man deprecates those speculations by means of which he had endeavoured to derive the knowledge of God's dominion and unity. It is thus that man becomes a servant, loving the object of his worship, and ready to perish for His sake, because he finds the sweetness of this attachment as great as the distress in the absence thereof. This forms a contrast to the philosophers, who see in the worship of God nothing but extreme refinement, extolling Him in truth above all other beings, just as the sun is placed on a higher level than the other visible things, and that the denial of God's existence is the mark of a low standard of the soul which delights in untruth.

16. Al Khazari: Now I understand the difference between Elohim and Adonai, and I see how far the God of Abraham is different from that of Aristotle. Man yearns for Adonai as a matter of love, taste, and conviction; whilst attachment to Elohim is the result of speculation. A feeling of the former kind invites its votaries to give their life for His sake, and to prefer death to His absence. Speculation, however, makes veneration only a necessity as long as it entails no harm, but bears no pain for its sake. I would, therefore, excuse Aristotle for thinking lightly about the observation of the law, since he doubts whether God has any cognizance of it.

17. The Rebbi: Abraham bore his burden honestly, viz. the life in Ur Kasdim, emigration, circumcision, the removal of Ishmael, and the distress of the sacrifice of Itzhak, because his share of the Divine Influence had come to him through love, but not through speculation. He observed that not the smallest detail could escape God, that he was quickly rewarded for his piety and guided on the right path to such an extent that he did everything in the order dictated by God. How could he do otherwise than deprecate his former speculation? The Sages explain the verse: And He brought him forth abroad, as meaning: give up thy horoscopy! That is to say, He commanded him to leave off his speculative researches into the stars and other matters, and to follow faithfully the object of his inclination, as it is written: Taste and see that the Lord is good. Adonai is, therefore, called rightly the God of Israel, because this view is not found among Gentiles. He is also called God of the land, because this possesses a special power in its air, soil and climate, which in connexion with the tilling of the ground, assists in improving the species. He who follows the divine law, follows the representatives of this view. His soul finds satisfaction in their teachings, in spite of the simplicity of their speech and ruggedness of their similes. This is not the case with the instructions of philosophers, with their eloquence and fine teachings, however great the impressiveness of their arguments. The masses do not follow them, because the human soul has a presentiment of the truth, as it is said: The words of truth will be recognised.

18. Al Khazari: I see thee turning against the philosophers, attributing to them things of which just the opposite is known. Of a person who lives in seclusion and acts rightly, it is said, he is a philosopher, and shares the views of philosophers. Thou deprivest them of every good action.

19. The Rebbi: Nay, what I told thee is the foundation of their belief, viz. that the highest human happiness consists in speculative science and in the conception by reason and thought of all intelligible matters. This is transformed into the active intellect, then, into emanating intellect, which is near the creative intellect without fear of decay. This cannot, however, be obtained except by devoting one's life to research and continual reflection, which is incompatible with worldly occupations. For this reason, they renounced wealth, rank, and the pleasure of children, in order not to be distracted from study. As soon as man has become acquainted with the final object of the knowledge sought for, he need not care what he does. They do not fear God for the sake of reward, nor do they think that if they steal or murder, they will be punished. They recommend good and dissuade from evil in the most admirable manner. And in order to resemble the Creator who arranged everything so perfectly, they have contrived laws, or rather regulations without binding force, and which may be overridden in times of need. The religious law, however, is not so except in its social parts, and the law itself sets down those which permit exceptions and those which do not.

20. Al Khazari: The light of which thou speakest has not gone out without hope of its being re-kindled. It has completely disappeared, and no one is able to trace it.

21. The Rebbi: It is only extinguished for him who does not see us with an open eye, who infers the extinction of our light from our degradation, poverty and dispersion, and concludes from the greatness of others, their conquests on earth and their power over us, that their light is still burning.

22. Al Khazari: I will not use this as an argument, as I see two antagonistic religions prevailing, although it is impossible that the truth should be on two opposite sides. It can only be on one or on neither. I have explained to thee in connexion with the verse: Behold My servant shall prosper, that humility and meekness are evidently nearer to the Divine Influence than glory and eminence. The same is visible in these two religions. Christians do not glory in kings, heroes and rich people, but in those who followed Jesus all the time, before His faith had taken firm root among them. They wandered away, or hid themselves, or were killed wherever one of them was found, suffered disgrace and slaughter for the sake of their belief. These are the people in whom they glory, whose ministers they revere, and in whose names, they build churches. In the same way did the **Helpers**, and friends of Islam bear much poverty, until they found assistance. In these, their humility and martyrdom do they glory; not in the princes who boasted of their wealth and power, but rather in those clad in rags and fed scantily on barley bread. Yet, O Jewish Rebbi, they did so in the utmost equanimity and devotion to God. Had I ever seen the Jews act in a like manner for the sake of God, I would place them above the kings of David's house. For I am well aware of what thou didst teach me concerning the words: 'with him also that is of a contrite and humble spirit, as well as that the light of God only rests upon the souls of the humble.

23. The Rebbi: Thou art right to blame us for bearing degradation without benefit. But if I think of prominent men amongst us who could escape this degradation by a word spoken lightly, become free men, and turn against their oppressors, but do not do so out of devotion to their faith: is not this the way to obtain intercession and remission of many sins? Should that which thou demandest of me really ever take place we should not remain in this condition. Besides this, God has a secret and wise design concerning us, which should be compared to the wisdom hidden in the seed which falls into the ground, where it undergoes an external transformation into earth, water and dirt, without leaving a trace for him who looks down upon it. It is, however, the seed itself which transforms earth and water into its own substance, carries it from one stage to another, until it refines the elements and transfers them into something like itself, casting off husks, leaves, etc., and allowing the pure core to appear, capable of bearing the Divine Influence. The original seed produced the tree bearing fruit resembling that from which it had been produced. In the same manner the law of Moshe transforms each one who honestly follows it, though it may externally repel him. The nations merely serve to introduce and pave the way for the expected MASHIACH, who is the fruition, and they will all become His fruit. Then, if they acknowledge Him, they will become one tree. Then they will revere the origin which they formerly dispersed, as we have observed concerning the words: "Behold My servant prospers." Consider not their abstention from idolatry, and energetic declaration of the unity of God, as a reason to praise; nor cast a reproving glance at the Israelites because their history tells of idol worship. On the other hand, consider that many of the former incline towards heresy and endeavour to spread it, that they praise it in popular songs which are in everybody's mouth, and which are loud in asserting that there is no king who rules over the actions of man, none who rewards or punishes them, a doctrine never mentioned in connexion with Israel. The people only sought to derive advantages from talismans and spirits, in addition to the practice of their faith of which they observed the laws, because the adoption of magic practices was universally prevalent at their time. Had this not been so, they should not have become converted to the belief of the peoples amongst whom they lived as exiles. Even Manasseh and Zedekiah and the greatest apostates in Israel had no particular wish to forsake the religion of Israel. They did it chiefly for victory and worldly gain which they hoped to obtain by means which they considered effective in spite of divine prohibition. If these things were so lightly considered to-day, thou wouldst see us and them deceived by them, as we are deceived by other vanities, such as astrology, conjuring, magic practices, and other tricks which are rejected as completely by nature as by the Law.

24. Al Khazari: I ask thee now to give me an explanation of the relics of the natural science which thou hast stated existed among you.

25. The Rebbi: To this belongs the **Book of Creation** by the Patriarch Abraham. Its contents are very profound, and require thorough explanation. It teaches the unity and omnipotence of God by means of various examples, which are multiform on one side and uniform on the other. They are in harmony with regard to the One, their director. This results in the three factors: **S'far**, **Sefer**, and **Sippur**. As to **S'far** it means the calculation and weighing of the created bodies. The calculation which is required for the harmonious and advantageous arrangement of a body is based on a numerical figure. Expansion, measure, weight, relation of movements, and musical harmony, all these are based on the number expressed by the word, **S'far**. No building emerges from the hand of the architect unless its image had first existed in his soul. Sippur signifies the language, or rather the divine language, the voice of the words of the living God. This produced the existence of the form which this language assumed in the words: Let there be light,' 'let there be a firmament. The word was hardly spoken, when the thing came into existence. This is also **Sefer**, by which writing is meant, the writing of God means His creatures, the speech of God is His writing, the will of God is His speech. In the nature of God, therefore, **S'far**, **Sippur**, and **Sefer** are a unity, whilst they are three in human reckoning. For man wills with his reason, speaks with his mouth, and writes such speech with his hand. These three factors characterize one of God's creatures. Man's will, writing, and word are marks of the thing, but not the nature of the same. The will, however, expressed in the word of God signifies the essence of the thing, and is at the same time His script. Imagine a silk weaver considering his work The silk obeys him, accepts the colours and patterns which he has contrived. The garment therefore comes into existence by his will and design. If we were able when speaking of, or drawing a human figure, to produce a human form, then we should have the word of God in our power and could create, just as we are able to do partially in forming objects in the mind. Spoken or written words have certain advantages over each other. In some cases, the name fits the object exactly; in others less so. The language created by God, which He taught Adam and placed on his tongue and in his heart, is without any doubt the most perfect and most fitted to express the things specified, as it is written: And whatsoever Adam called every living creature, that was the name thereof. This means that it deserved such name which fitted and characterized it. This shows the excellence of the 'holy tongue' as well as the reason why the angels employed it in preference to any other. Writing is judged from a similar point of view. The shapes of the letters are not the result of accident, but of a device which is in harmony with the character of each letter. Thou shouldst not, now, deem it impossible that names and combinations of letters, whether spoken or written, have certain effects. In either case, calculation, viz. the thought of the pure, angelic soul precedes the act. Thus the three factors: **S'far**, Sippur, and Sefer become a unity, and the calculation appears as if a being, endowed with a pure soul, had made, spoken, and written it. The book further states with regard to God: He created His world with three **Sefirah** factors: **S'far**, **Sippur**, and **Sefer**. In God's nature they are all one, but this one forms the beginning of the thirty-two miraculous and mysterious ways of the divine wisdom, composed of the ten **Sefiroth** and the twenty-two letters of the Hebrew alphabet. This points to the actuality of existing things and their differences with regard to quantity and quality. Quantity means a number. The mystery of the number is in the number ten, as is expressed in the passage: **Ten Sefiroth** without anything else; ten and not nine, ten and not eleven. A deep secret lies in the fact that the counting stops at ten, neither more nor less. The next sentence, therefore, runs: 'Understand judiciously and judge intelligently, examine and search them, mind, weigh, and consider, render everything lucid, and place the Creator in His sphere; their measure is ten in endless progression. This is followed by a division as to quality. The twenty-two letters are divided into three groups, viz. three mothers, seven double, twelve single consonants. The three mothers are alef, mem, shin. They cover a great and profound secret; for from them emanate air, water, and fire by means of which the universe was created. The grouping of these consonants united with the order of the macrocosm and the microcosm, viz. man, and the order of time into one line, called 'true witnesses, viz. universe, soul, year. This also demonstrates that the one order is the work of a one-Master, who is God. And although things are multifarious and different from each other, their difference is the result of the difference of their material, which is partly of higher and partly lower order, and of impure or pure character. The giver of forms, designs and order, however, has placed in them all a unique wisdom, and a providence which is in complete harmony with this uniform order, and is visible in the macrocosm, in man, and in the arrangement of the spheres. It is this that is called the **true witnesses** of His Oneness, viz. universe, soul, year. This yields approximately the following table-

Three Mothers: AM"S
In the Universe: Air, Water, Fire.
In the Soul: Chest, Belly, Head.
In the Year: Moisture, Cold, Heat.
Seven Double Consonants. Beth, Gimel, Daleth, Kaf, Pe, Resh, Tav.
In the Universe: Saturnus, Jupiter, Mars, Sun, Venus, Mercury, Moon.
In the Soul: Wisdom, Wealth, Government, Life, Grace, Progeny, Peace.
In the Year: Sabbath, Thursday, Tuesday,

Kuzari — Fourth Essay

Sunday, Friday, Wednesday, Monday.

Twelve Simple Consonants: [ה ו ז ח ט י ל נ ס ע צ ק]

In the Universe: Aries, Taurus, Gemini, Cancer, Leo, Virgo, Libra, Scorpio, Arcitenens, Caper, Amphora, Pisces.

In the Soul: Organs of Sight, Hearing, Smelling, Speaking, Tasting, Feeling, Organs of Working, Walking, Thinking, Being Angry, of Laughing, and Sleeping.

In the Year: Nisan, Iyyar, Sivan, Tammuz, Ab, Ellul, Tishri, Marheshwan, Kislev, Tebeth, Shebat Adar.

One upon three, three upon seven, and seven upon twelve. All these organs have one spot in common. counselling kidneys, laughing spleen angry liver, sleeping stomach. It cannot be denied that the kidneys have the faculty of giving good advice, as we know a similar circumstance to be connected with other organs. A eunuch is of weaker intelligence than a woman; both lack the beard and sound judgment. The spleen is called 'laughing' because it is its nature to cleanse both blood and spirit from unclean and obscuring matter. If they are pure, cheerfulness and laughing arise. The **angry liver** is so termed on account of the gall which takes its origin from it. **Stomach** is the name for the digestive organs. The heart is not mentioned because it is the principal organ, neither are the diaphragm and the lung, because they serve the heart especially, but the rest of the body only incidentally, and were not originally so intended. The brain's task is to collect the different senses connected with it. The organs which are situated below the diaphragm have another secret, because they represent primary nature. The diaphragm separates the physical world from the animal one, just as the neck separates the animal world from the rational one, as Plato points out in the Timaeus. Primary matter originates in the physical world, and here is to be found the origin of existence. From here the seed is sent forth and the embryo produced out of the four elements. Here also God selected the parts which are used as offerings, viz. fat, blood, the caul above the liver, and the two kidneys. He selected neither the heart, nor the brain, nor the lung, nor the diaphragm. This is a most profound secret, the lifting of which is prohibited. It is therefore taught: One should not examine the work of creatio except under rare circumstances. The book says further: Seven double consonants, six plains for the six sides, and the holy Temple placed in the middle. Blessed be He from His place; He is the Place of the universe, but the universe is not His place. This is an allusion to the Divine Influence which unites the contrasts. The book compares Him to the central point of a body, with six sides and three dimensions. As long as the centre is not fixed, the sides cannot be fixed. Attention is further called to the relation between these and the power which bears the universe, and through which contrasts are united by eliciting comparisons between Universe, Soul, and Year. To each of these a something is given which comprehends and arranges its component parts. The dragon in the universe is as a king on his throne; the sphere in the year is as a king in the country; the heart in the soul is as a king in war. **Dragon** is the name of the moon sphere, and is employed as an appellation for the world of reason, because things hidden and imperceptible by the senses are called dragon. The 'sphere' relates to the ecliptic of the sun sphere, because it regulates the seasons of the year. The **heart** regulates the animal life, and directs its divisions. The meaning of the whole is that the wisdom visible in all three is one, and the Divine Influence is one, whilst the difference existing between them is based on the difference of matter. The authority ruling the spiritual world is compared to a king on his throne, whose commands, or even smallest hints, are obeyed by his servants, high and low, who know him, without any movement on his part or on theirs. When directing the spheres, he is compared to the king in the country. For he must show himself at the borders in order that all parts should see him as a redoubtable and benevolent ruler. When controlling the animal world, he is compared to a king in war, who is swayed by contradictory feelings; he wishes success to his friends and defeat to his enemies. Wisdom, however, is one only. But the wisdom displayed in the spheres is not greater than in the smallest animals. The former, it is true, is of a higher class, because it consists of pure and lasting matter which cannot be destroyed except by its Creator, whilst animals are made from a matter which is susceptible to contradictory influences, such as heat, cold, and others which affect its nature. Time would have destroyed them, had not Providence instituted the masculine and feminine principles in order to preserve the species, in spite of the decay of the individual. This is a consequence of the revolution of the sphere as well as of the rising and setting of the heavenly bodies. The book calls attention to this circumstance, and says that there is no physical difference between woman and man except certain external and internal organs. Anatomy teaches that the female genitals are but the inverted male ones. The book expresses this thus: Man is alef, mem, shin; woman is alef, shin, mem; the wheel turns forwards and backwards; nothing better above than pleasure, nothing worse below than injury. This means that the letter groups alef, mem, shin, and alef, shin, mem; 'aynh, nun, gimel, and nun, gimel, ayn are always the same, only differently grouped, just as the rising and setting of the sphere remain stationary, only appearing to us to move forwards and backwards. Then the book allegorises the human organs in the following manner: Two mumbling, two rejoicing, two counselling, two jubilant. He put them in contrast, placed them in opposition, one part of one side being allied to one of the other, standing up for each other, or against one another; some are nothing without others, but all are linked to each other. The allusion is clear when considered in its entirety, however difficult it may be to explain it in detail, to explain that the animal needs contrasts, that its preservation is the result of this strife, and that it could not exist without the latter. Counting up the creatures which are headed by the noblest, viz. spirit of the living God, the book goes on to say: Firstly, the spirit of the living God; secondly, air emanating from the spirit; thirdly, water from the wind; fourthly, fire from water. The earth element is not mentioned, because it forms the gross material of the creatures which are all made of earth. One says rather: This is a fiery body, or an atmospheric one, or an aqueous one. For this reason, the three mothers, fire, water, and air, are placed in front, but they are preceded by the spirit of God, which is the Holy Ghost, of which were created the angels and with which the soul is connected. After this comes the perceptible atmosphere, then the water which is above the firmament, and neither grasped nor acknowledged by philosophic speculation. A solution might be found in the circumstance that this is the zone of intense cold which forms the limit of the clouds. Above this is the ether, which is the place of the elementary fire, as the book hath it: Fire from water, or as the Torah says: And the spirit of God moved upon the face of the water. This water is the primary matter, not qualified, but tohu wabohu, which, by the encompassing will of God, assumed a certain character and the name **Spirit of God**. The comparison of the primary matter with water is most suitable, because no compact substance can arise from a material which is finer than water. But a substance which is of greater density than water does not, on account of this density, admit the influences of nature. Earthly matter alone can be wrought, because in handling it only the surfaces of the material are concerned, but not all its particles. Nature however, penetrates the atoms. There is consequently no product of nature which did not, at one time, exist in a liquid condition. If this had not been so, it could not have been called a natural, but only an artificial coinpound, or accidental formation. Nature can only exercise her influence on liquid matters, which she can form at her will, but leave alone as soon as it is necessary for them to become hard. Concerning this the book says: He made substance from chaos, and the non-existent existing. He carved great pillars from intangible air. Further: Water from air; he has carved and hewn tohu and bohu, mud and clay;

Kuzari — Fourth Essay

he made them into a kind of flower bed, raised them like a wall, covered them like a floor, poured water over them, and they became dust. Tohu is the green line which surrounds the whole universe. Bohu are the mud-covered stones which are submerged in the ocean, and from between which water comes forth.' In the following portions light is shed on the secret of the holy name, viz. the Tetragrammaton, which corresponds to the nature of the One God, which is without quiddity. For the quiddity of a thing is outside its essence, whilst the existence of God is identical with His quiddity. The quiddity of a thing is its definition, and the latter is composed of the species and divisibility of the thing defined. The primary cause, however, has neither species nor divisibility. He therefore can be nothing but He. The book, then, shows that the revolution of the sphere is the cause of the variety of things, in the following words: The wheel turns forward and backward. This is compared to the combination of single letters, viz. alef placed in combination with all the others, all the others with alef; beth with all the others, all the others with beth. This continued through the whole alphabet results in two hundred and thirty-one combinations. The variety would be greater in groups of three and four letters [which is expressed in the following formula]: 'Three stones build six houses; four stones build four-and-twenty houses; go and calculate that which

Kuzari — Fourth Essay

the human mouth cannot express nor the ear hear.' An inquiry is also necessary into how things multiplied prior to the revolution of the sphere, the Creator being One, whilst the sphere, so to speak, has six sides. The book, then, in spiritual language, finds a name for the Creator, choosing, in order to express it in physical speech, the slenderest consonants which are as a breath in comparison to the other letters, viz. he, waw, yod. The book says that the divine will, when going forth under this great name, carries out everything God wishes. There is no doubt that He and the angels speak that spiritual language, and knew, even before the world was created, everything that was to happen in the physical world, as well as how speech and intelligence would emanate from Him on mankind, which was to be created in the world. From this it follows that the physical world was created in a manner congruous to the tangible element of the holy and spiritual name, which, in its turn, is congruous to the tangible name, YHW, YWH, HWY, HYW, WYH, WHY. Each of these groups was responsible for one direction of the universe, and thus arose the sphere. This, however, is not satisfactory, because the object of research is either too profound to be fathomed, or our minds are inadequate, or for both reasons simultaneously. Philosophers speculating on these things arrive at the conclusion that from one only one can issue. They conjectured an angel, standing near

Kuzari — Fourth Essay

to God, and having emanated from the Prime Cause. To this angel they attributed two characteristics; firstly, his consciousness of his own existence by his very essence; secondly, his consciousness of having a cause. Two things resulted from this, viz. an angel and the sphere of fixed stars. From his recognition of the Prime Cause a second angel emanated, and from his consciousness of his existence emanated the sphere of Saturnus, and so forth to the moon, and the Creative Intellect. People accepted this theory, and were deceived by it to such an extent, that they looked upon it as conclusive, because it was attributed to Greek philosophers. It is, however, a mere assertion without convincing power, and open to various objections. Firstly, for what reason did this emanation cease; did the Prime Cause become impotent? Secondly, it might be asked: Why, from Saturnus' recognition of what was above, did not one thing arise, and from his recognition of the first angel another thing, so that the Saturnine emanations counted four? Whence do we know altogether that if a being became conscious of its essence a sphere must arise, and from the recognition of the Prime Cause, an angel must arise? When Aristotle asserts that he was conscious of his existence, one may consistently expect that a sphere should emanate from him, and when he asserts that he recognised the Prime Cause, an angel should emanate. I communicated these rudiments to thee lest philosophers confuse thee and thou think that by following it thou might satisfy thy soul with a clear demonstration. These rudiments are as unacceptable to reason as they are extravagant in the face of logic. Neither do two philosophers agree on this point, unless they be disciples of the same teacher. But Empedocles, Pythagoras, Aristotle, Plato, and many others entirely disagree with each other.

26. Al Khazari: Why should the letters **H W Y** or an angel or a sphere or other things be required if we believe in the Divine will and creation, and if we believe that God created the immense variety of things and species in one moment, as is related in the Book of Genesis- that He placed in everything the faculty of preservation and propagation, and sustains them every moment by His divine power? Do we not say: His bounty renews every day for ever, the work of creation.

27. The Rebbi: Just so, O King of the Khazars, by God! This is the truth, the real faith, and everything else may be abandoned. Perhaps this was Abraham's point of view when divine power and unity dawned upon him prior to the revelation accorded to him. As soon as this took place, he gave up all his speculations and only strove to gain favour of God, having ascertained what this was and how and where it could be obtained. The Sages explain the words: And he brought him forth abroad. thus: Give up thy horoscopy, This means: Forsake astrology as well as any other doubtful study of nature. Plato relates that a prophet, who lived at the time of the king Morinus, said prophetically to a philosopher who was zealously devoted to his art: Thou canst not reach me on this road, but only those whom I have placed as intermediaries between me and mankind, viz. the prophets and the true law. The Book of Yetzirah is constructed on the mystery of ten units equally acknowledged in east and west, but neither from natural causes, nor rational conviction. The following sentences are a Divine mystery: Ten Sefiroth without anything else; close thy mouth from speaking, close thy heart from thinking. If thy heart runs away, return to God; for with reference to this [the prophet] says: Running and returning. On this basis the covenant was made. Their measure is ten in endless progression, the end being linked to the beginning, and the beginning to the end just as a flame which is attached to the coal. Know thou, think and reflect that the Creator is one, without another, and there is no number which thou canst count before **one**. The book concludes as follows: As soon as Abraham had understood, meditated, discerned and clearly grasped, the Lord of the universe revealed

Kuzari — Fourth Essay

Himself to him, called him His friend and made a covenant with him between the ten fingers of his hand, which is the covenant of the tongue; and between the ten toes of his feet, which is the covenant of circumcision, and He pronounced upon him the word: Before I formed thee in the belly, I knew thee.

28. Al Khazari: Give me now an idea of the Sages accomplishments in natural science.

29. The Rebbi: I have already called thy attention to the fact that they were so skilled in real astronomical observations that they knew the revolution of the moon which, according to Davidian tradition, amounts to twenty-nine days, twelve hours and seven hundred and ninety-three fractions. No flaw has been found in it hitherto. They also calculated the solar year, taking care that Passover should not fall till after the **Tekufah** of Nisan [**Tekufot** [Hebrew: תקופות, singular: tekufah, literally, **Turn** or Cycle, are the four seasons of the year recognized by Talmud writers. According to Samuel Yarḥinai, each tekufah marks the beginning of a period of 91 days 7½ hours. The four tekufot are: A. Tekufat Nisan, the vernal equinox, when the sun enters Aries; this is the beginning of spring, or **Eit hazera** [seed-time], when day and night are equal. B. Tekufat Tammuz, the summer solstice, when the sun enters Cancer; this is the summer season, or Et

ha-katsir [harvest-time], when the day is the longest in the year. C. Tekufat Tishrei, the autumnal equinox, when the sun enters Libra, and autumn, or **Et ha-batsir** [vintage-time], begins, and when the day again equals the night. D. Tekufat Tevet, the winter solstice, when the sun enters Capricornus; this is the beginning of winter, or **Et ha-ḥoref** [winter-time], when the night is the longest during the year], as some of them explained: If you see that the equinox of Nisan would be on the sixteenth of Nisan, make the year an embolismic one, lest Passover fell in the winter season. God's command fixed the feast in the words: Observe the month of Abib. The **Tekufah**, as accepted by the people, is not the true one, but only approximate, on account of the division of the year into four seasons, viz. ninety-one days, seven and a half hours. According to this calculation Passover would fall in the winter. This induced the Christians to attack the Jews and to think that the latter had lost the basis of their belief. They themselves are without a basis, since their Easter would, according to their calculation of the commonly known equinox, take place before the beginning of spring. They did not, however, pay attention to the true equinox, which was kept secret and not given up to common knowledge. According to their calculation Passover never falls otherwise than when the sun has reached the head of Aries, though only by one day. For the last thousand years no mistake has occurred, and this agrees with the calculation of Al Battani, being most correct and accurate. Can the revolutions of sun and moon be calculated otherwise than by a most intimate knowledge of astronomy. The problem of the sentence: If the new moon appears before noon, etc... has been discussed before. There exists a book on this special subject, styled Chapters of Rebbi Eliezer, in which we find dissertations on the extent of the globe and every sphere, the nature of the stars, the signs of the zodiac, constellations, houses, happy omens, good and evil influences, ascensions and descensions, elevations and the extent of their movements. He was one of the best-known doctors of the Mishnah. Samuel, one of the doctors of the Talmud said: The roads of heaven are as familiar to me as the streets of Nehardaea. They devoted themselves to this study only in the service of the Law, because the calculation of the revolution of the moon with the disturbances of her course did not completely tally with the calculation of the time of her conjunction with the sun, viz., the Molad. The time when the moon is not visible prior to the Molad and immediately after it also, can only be calculated with the help of sound astronomical knowledge. Similarly, the knowledge of the changes of the four seasons can only be properly obtained with the aid of a knowledge of the lowest and highest points and the various ascensions of stars as well as their variations. He who occupies himself with this study must bring to bear on it also the knowledge of spheres. The remarkable knowledge of natural history displayed in the sayings of the Sages, without any intention on their part of teaching this science, is quite astonishing. What books, in thy opinion, must have been at the disposal even of the students among them.

30. Al Khazari: I wonder how it is that the books written for the purpose were lost whilst these incidental sayings were saved.

31. The Rebbi: Because their contents were retained in the minds of a few people, only one of whom was an astronomer, another a physician or an anatomist. If a nation perishes it is first the higher classes which disappear, and literature with them. There only remain the law books which the people require, know by heart, copy and preserve. Whatever element of those sciences was embodied in the Talmudical law codes was thus protected and preserved by the zeal of many students. To these belong everything appertaining to the rules for slaughtering cattle, or making them unlawful to be eaten. A large amount of this remained unknown to Galen If this were not so, why does he not mention easily recognisable diseases to which the Law calls attention. Among these are diseases of the lungs and heart, growths on the latter and on its sides, the growing together of the lobes of the lung, deficiency or redundance of the same, or if they are dried up or lacerated. Their acquaintance with the vital and vegetative organs is shown in the following sentence: The brain has two skins to which correspond two on the testicles. Two bean-shaped growths are situated at the lower end of the skull; inside them is the brain, outside is the spine. Further: There are three arteries; one leads to the heart, the second to the lung, and the third to the liver. They distinguished between fatal diseases and less dangerous ones in the following words: If the skin of the spine is preserved, the marrow remains intact. He whose marrow becomes soft cannot beget children. Further: a skin formed in consequence of a wound on the lung is no real skin. The regulation concerning the 'sinew that shrinks' does not apply to birds, because they have no hollow of the hip. Worth mentioning are the following regulations: The contents of the stomach of a lawful animal suckled by an unlawful one is unlawful, but the contents of the stomach of an unlawful animal suckled by a lawful one are lawful, because the milk becomes compact in the entrails. Very profound, though beyond our grasp, is the following prohibition: Five cuticles are unlawful, viz. that of the brain, testicles, spleen, kidneys and lower end of the spine, all these it is unlawful to eat. They have also very skilfully determined the height from which a fall would make an animal unlawful on account of shattering of limbs, which means the tearing of limbs which endangers its life. They say as follows: If one has left an animal above a structure, and finds it below, shattering of limbs is not to be feared, because the animal measures itself, which means that the animal measures and prepares for the leap, without damage. This would not be the case if it were pushed. Leaping is assisted by presence of mind, whilst a push produces fear. The following regulation is also interesting: The naturally reduced lung is lawful, the artificially reduced one is unlawful on account of 'shrinking.' This can be examined by keeping it in tepid water for four and twenty hours. If it re-assumes a healthy appearance, it is lawful, but not otherwise. If the lung has the colour of antimony, it is lawful, if it is like ink it is unlawful, because this blackness is a morbid transformation of red. The yellow lung is lawful. If a lung is partially red, it is lawful, but unlawful if it is completely red. A child of a yellowish tint was brought before Rebbi **Nathan of Babylon** who decided: Wait until the blood has gone down. He meant to say that the circumcision should not take place till the blood had spread through the whole body. This was done and the life of the child was saved, although other children of the same mother had died soon after the circumcision. Subsequently a child was brought before of a reddish hue, and he said: 'Wait till the blood has been absorbed.' The child was saved in consequence and was called after him: **Nathan Habbabli**. They further said: Lawful fat can close up an internal wound, but not unlawful fat. A very acute decision is the following: If a needle is found in the thick wall of the stomach together with a drop of blood, [it must have entered before the animal was killed] if no blood is visible, it must have entered afterwards. The issue of this effects the validity of the sale, because after the killing no blood could approach the needle, as the blood does not flow in a dead animal. The buyer cannot, therefore, return the animal to the seller. If, however, blood is found, he can return it with the plea: Thou hast sold me an animal liable to die. A scab on a wound shows that the latter was three days old before the animal was killed, if no scab is to be seen the plaintiff must bring other evidence. The characteristics of a clean bird are the following: Place the bird on a stretched rope; if it divides its claws two by two, it is an unclean bird, if it divides them three by one, it is a clean one. Further: Every bird that catches its food in the air is unclean, a bird that lives with notoriously unclean ones, as the starling among ravens, is of the same character. A symptom of birth among small cattle is a flow of blood; among big cattle after-birth; in a woman: placenta and after-birth. Very strange are the sayings concerning the poison contained in the claws of certain animals: a cat, a sparrow-hawk, and martin strike poison into kids and lambs; the weasel wounds birds. The fox and the dog convey no poison. This poisoning is conveyed by the claw, but not by the teeth; only by the forefoot, but not by the hindfoot; only when the animal does it purposely, and is alive. All this means that an animal can only poison any other by striking it purposely, but not accidentally, or if the claw remains sticking in the flesh without any tearing intention. The addition 'living animal' is therefore most remarkable. For it the striking foot were cut off and the claw remained in the flesh of the wound of the other animal, no poisoning takes place, because the poison is not conveyed till the claw is withdrawn for this reason the words 'while living are placed intentionally after 'on purpose. They say further: If the liver is missing excepting the size of an olive near the gall, its natural place, the animal is lawful. Matter is harmless on the lung, but not on the kidneys. Clear water and a hole are harmless on the kidney but fatal for the lungs. If an animal has been skinned, a piece as large as a coin remaining on the spine suffices to make the animal lawful. The Mishnah also contains regulations concerning unlawful food, defects of first-born animals, defects of priests, too many to enumerate, not to speak of commenting on them. Apart from this the anatomy of the skeleton is given in very concise, yet clear description. An admirable saying is: If the intestines protrude, but show no hole, the animal is lawful. This, however, the Mishnah adds, is only the case if they have not been inverted. If this has taken place, the animal is unlawful; for it is written: He has made thee and established thee, which means that God has created man as a well-established being. If one of his organs were inverted, he could not live. The Sages further distinguish the various appearances of blood of issue or wounds and haemorrhoids, the rules of menstruation and male issue, symptoms of leprosy, and other matters too deep for our capacity.

Kuzari   Fourth Essay

Fifth Essay

1. AL KHAZARI: I must trouble thee to give me a clear and concise discourse on religious principles and axioms according to the method of the Mutakallims. Let me hear them exactly as thou didst study them, that I may accept or refute them. Since I have not been granted a perfect faith free from doubts, and I was formerly sceptical, had my own opinions, and exchanged ideas with philosophers and followers of other religions, I consider it most advantageous to learn and to instruct myself how to refute dangerous and foolish views. Tradition in itself is a good thing if it satisfies the soul, but a perturbed soul prefers research, especially if examination leads to the verification of tradition. Then knowledge and tradition become united.

2. The Rebbi: Where is the soul which is strong enough not to be deceived by the views of philosophers, scientists, astrologers, adepts, magicians, materialists, and others, and can adopt a belief without having first passed through many stages of heresy? Life is short, but labour long. Only few there are to whom belief comes naturally, who avoid all these views, and whose soul always detects the points of error in them. I hope that thou art one of those few. Since I cannot resist, I will not lead thee the way of the Karaites, who ascended the heights of metaphysics without intermediate steps. I will give thee a clear standpoint, which will assist thee to acquire clear notions of matter and form, elements, nature, soul, intellect, and metaphysics in general. After this I will prove to thee, as briefly as possible, that the rational soul can exist without a body; further, the existence of reward hereafter, providence and omnipotence. As regards tangible objects, we can perceive their quantity and quality by means of our senses, whilst reason maintains that they are borne by a fulcrum which is difficult to imagine. How can we imagine a thing that has neither quantity nor quality. Imagination denies its existence, but reason answers that quantity and quality are accidents which have no independent existence, but must necessarily have an object to support them. Philosophers call this object matter, adding that our intelligence grasps its meaning only imperfectly, since imperfection is its nature; that it does not really exist, and therefore cannot claim any predicate, and although it only exists virtually, its predicate is corporeal. Aristotle says that it is, so to speak, ashamed to appear naked, and therefore only shows itself clothed in a form. Some people believe that the 'water' spoken of in the biblical account of the creation is an appellation for this matter, and that 'the spirit of the Lord hovering over the surface of the water' only expresses the divine will which penetrates all atoms of matter, with which He does what, how, and when He desires, as the potter with the shapeless clay. The absence of form and order is called darkness and tohu wabohu. After this the wise, divine will ordained the revolution of the uppermost sphere, which completes one revolution in four and twenty hours, carrying all other spheres with it. Through this the matter which fills the sphere of the moon underwent a change, which was in accordance with the movements of the spheres. The first process was that the air near the moon sphere became hot, because it was nearest to the periphery. It thus became an aetherial fire, called elementary fire by natural philosophers, having neither colour nor combustion, and being a fine, delicate, and light substance. It is called the fire sphere. Then comes the water sphere, and then the terrestrial globe, which forms a heavy and compact centre, being removed farthest from the periphery. These are the four elements, from the intermixture of which all things arise.

3. Al Khazari: In the opinion of philosophers, as I see, things arise by accident, since they say that that which happened to be nearest to the sphere became fire, and what was remotest became earth, whilst the middle part, according to proximity either to the periphery or to the centre, became air or water.

4. The Rebbi: Yet necessity forces them to acknowledge a divine wisdom in the distinction of one element from the other. The fire element is not distinguished from the atmospheric element, the latter from that of water, and the aqueous one from the terrestrial one by quantity or strength, but by the form specific to each; one is made into fire, another into air, the third into water, and the last into earth, otherwise one might say that the whole sphere is filled up with earthy matter, but that one portion was finer than another. Another may assert that it is all fire, only the lower parts are denser and cooler. We see that the spheres of the elements touch one another, but each preserves its form and speciality. We see how air, water and earth are in contact in one place without absorbing each other, till they are transformed one into another by other causes. Water assumes the form of air, air the form of fire, and then the element justly takes the other's name. Since substances, apart from. their accidences, are distinguished by their forms, philosophers found it correct to assert the activity of a divine creative intellect which bestows these forms, just as it bestowed them to plants and animals, which are all composed of the four elements. The vine and palm are not distinguished by accidental qualities, but by forms which made the substance of one different from the substance of the other. Accidental qualities would only distinguish one vine from another, and one palm from another, one, being black, the other one white, one sweeter, one longer or shorter, one thicker or thinner than the other. The forms of substances have no quantity; one horse cannot be less equine than another, nor one man more human than another, because the definitions 'equine' and 'human' are common to each individual horse and man. Philosophers involuntarily acknowledged that these forms could only be given by the Divine Influence, which they call form-giving Intelligence.

5. Al Khazari: This, as thou livest, is belief, considering that reason forces us to acknowledge such a thing. How can we now speak of accidents, or why do we not say that he who made this being a horse, and the other a man, by wisdom incomprehensible in detail, is the same who made fire fire, and earth earth through a wisdom beheld by God, but not by accidental proximity to or distance from the sphere.

6. The Rebbi: This is the religious argument. Evidence of it is to be found in the Children of Israel, for whose sake changes in nature were wrought, as well as new things created. If this evidence be removed, thy opponent and thou might agree that a vine, grew in this place because a seed happened to have fallen there. The seed assumed its form only by accident, because the revolution of the sphere resulted in a constellation which caused a mixture of elements productive of what thou now seest.

7. Al Khazari: I should refer my opponent to the uppermost sphere and its mover, and ask him whether or not, this is the result of accident. I should further refer him to the spherical constellations, which are unlimited. We see, however, that the number of forms of animal and plant life is not unlimited, allowing neither increase nor diminution. One might think that new constellations would produce new formations, and that others would perish.

8. The Rebbi: This is all the more correct, as with regard to many we understand their inherent wisdom as well as purpose, just as Aristotle explained in his discourse on -The utility of the species of animals, or Galen in - The utility of the organs,' not to speak of other wonderful achievements of the divine wisdom. In the instance of domestic animals, such as sheep, cattle, horses and asses, it is clear that they were created for the benefit of man. For in a wild state, they are imperfect, but useful when domesticated. David's allusion in the words: How great are Thy works, O Lord, serves to refute Epicurus' view that the universe arose by accident.

9. Al Khazari: Although it may be a digression, explain the meaning of this psalm to me.

10. The Rebbi: It runs parallel with the history of creation. The words: He who covereth Himself with light, correspond to - Let there be light, and there was light. The words: He stretcheth out the heavens like a carpet, run parallel to 'Let there be a firmament'; the words: He who layette the beams. to - the water above the firmament. He then describes the atmospheric phenomena, clouds, winds, fires, lightnings, and thunder, which all stand under God's guidance, as it is written: For by them judgeth He the people. In the psalm this is described in the words: 'He who maketh the clouds His chariot, who walketh upon the wings of the winds, who maketh the winds His messengers, and His ministers a flaming fire. This means that He dispatches them whither and on what errand He desires. Thus far the phenomena of the atmosphere. The psalm, then, passes on to - let the waters... be gathered... and the dry land appear, which is parallel to: 'He founded the earth on its bases.' According to its nature water would close up above the earth, covering it completely, hills and dales, like a garment, as the psalm hath it: 'With the flood, as with a robe, thou coveredst it; waters stand above the mountains.' Divine Providence, however, obviated its natural inclination, and sent it down to the ocean's deep, to let animals arise and God's wisdom appear. The words: At Thy rebuke they flee, describe the retirement of the water in the seas and underneath the earth. The same condition is alluded to in the words: 'To Him that spread out the earth above the water, a sentence which seemingly contradicts the other: 'With the flood as with a robe Thou coveredst it, the latter corresponding to the nature of the water, whilst the former describes God's wisdom and omnipotence. Then the psalm continues: Thou didst appoint a bound, that they might not pass over, nor turn again to cover the earth. All this is intended for the benefit of mankind. By means of certain clever works and dykes man keeps off the floods of rivers, utilising only so much water as is required for mills and irrigation. The psalm now says: He sends forth springs into the valleys, that they should, give drink to every beast of the plain, as soon as the wild beasts were created. The words: Upon them dwell the birds of the heaven. Refer to the creation of the birds. The psalm, then, passes on to 'Let the earth bring forth. In the words: To the mountains He gives drink from His upper chambers. This is only another expression for: But there went up a mist from the earth. likewise for the benefit of Adam and his posterity. The psalm says: 'He causes grass to spring up for the cattle, lest the grass be despised, since it is of service for the domestic animals, oxen, sheep, and horses. This is described in the words: **Service of man**, viz. agriculture, by means of which he produces corn for himself, as is expressed in the words: 'To bring forth bread from the earth. This is parallel to the verse: 'Behold, I have given you every herb bearing seed, viz. the corn for man, and the chaff for the rest of creatures, as it is said: 'And to every beast of the earth, and to every fowl of the heaven... every green herb for meat. The psalm then mentions the three foods gained from the soil, viz. corn, wine and oil, which are comprised in the term leḥem, and their usages as follows: Wine which gladdens man's heart, to make his face shine more than oil, and bread, - viz. the loaf-sustains man's heart. Then he mentions the importance of rain for the trees in the words: 'The trees of the Lord have their fill. These high trees have a use for some animals, as is expressed in the words: Wherein the birds make their nests, just as the high mountains serve other animals, viz. 'The high mountains are for the wild goats, the crags a refuge for the coneys.' Thus far the description of the dry land. The psalm then discusses the Biblical words: **Let there be lights** as follows: The moon He made to measure time. After this is mentioned the utility of the night which is not the work of accident, but of intention. There is no trifling in His work, nor even in the accidental consequences of the same. The night is but the

Kuzari — Fifth Essay

time of the absence of sunlight, yet instituted for a purpose. This is expressed in the words: 'Thou makest darkness, and it is night. This is followed by the description of beasts dangerous to man, which go forth at night and hide by day, whilst man and domestic animals sleep at night and walk abroad during the day. 'Man goes forth to his work and to his labour until the evening. Having thus included all terrestrial animals in the discussion of the rivers and heavenly lights, and having also mentioned man, there only remain the animals which live in water, the life of which is very little known to us, because Divine Wisdom lavished on them is not so manifest to us as in the former. Speaking of the wisdom which is visible, the psalmist breaks out in praise and says: How manifold are Thy works, O Lord. He then resumes the subject of the ocean and what is therein, concluding with the words: 'Let the glory of the Lord endure for ever; let the Lord rejoice in His works. This is a rendering of the words: 'And God saw everything that He had made, and behold it was very good. At the same time, it is an allusion to the seventh day in the words: **He rested, He blessed, He sanctified**, because it marked the completion of the works of nature, which had a time limit, and placed man on a par with angels, which, being spirits, are above natural impulses, and not bound by time in their works. Intellect can, as we see, picture heaven and earth in one moment. This is the world of celestial life and bliss where the soul finds ease at the moment when it reaches it. The Sabbath is, therefore, called 'a taste of the world to come.'-Let us now resume the discussion on the opinion held by philosophers that the elements having entered various combinations relative to the variety of climes, atmosphere, and constellations, received a variety of forms from the Giver of forms. All minerals are, therefore, but the sum total of the specific powers and faculties. Others assert that the powers and qualities of minerals are the product of combination only, and consequently do not require forms of divine origin. The latter are only necessary for plants and animals to which a soul is attributed. The finer this mixture is, the nobler is the form proper for it in which the divine wisdom manifests itself in a higher degree. It becomes a plant which is possessed of some feeling and perception, penetrates the earth, and derives nourishment from good, moist soil and sweet water, avoiding the contrast. Thus, it grows, until it comes to a stand-still, having given life to another like it and produced seed. This seed, then, according to a wisdom implanted in it, pursues a similar course. Philosophers call this nature, or rather powers which guard the preservation of the species, since the essence of the individual cannot be preserved, it being composed of various component parts. A thing which possesses these powers of growth, propagation and nourishment, is devoid of the power of motion, and is, in the opinion of philosophers, guided by nature. As a matter of fact, it is God who controls it in a certain condition. Call this condition what thou wilt, nature, soul, power, or angel. If the mixture is still finer, and fit to be impressed by the divine wisdom, it is favoured with a higher form than the bare physical power. It is able to bring its food from a distance, and is possessed of organs subject to it, which cannot move except by its desire. It has more control over its parts than the plant with which the wind plays, which cannot ward off damage, nor obtain what is useful to it. The animal has limbs to move about from place to place. The form allotted to it above its physical life is called soul. The souls vary greatly according to the preponderance of one or the other of the four elements. The wisdom of Providence has also constituted each living being for the benefit of the whole world. We may not be aware of the use of most of them, any more than we know of the use of ships' implements, and consider them therefore useless, whilst the master and builder of the ship knows it. We would not know the purpose of many of our bones and other organs if they lay detached before us, and so we are in ignorance of the purpose of every bone and limb, although we use it, and are convinced that if we lacked one, our actions would be impaired, and we could not do without it. All atoms of the world are known to, and mustered by, their Creator, and nothing can be added to it, nor anything taken away from it. It is necessary that souls should differ from each other, and that the organs of each soul should be suitable to it. For this reason, He endowed the lion with organs for seizing its prey, such as teeth and claws, in addition to courage; but to the hart He gave the means of flight as compensation for its timidity. Every soul instinctively uses its faculties according to their nature, but nature does not reach perfection in any part of animal life, and consequently has no desire to obtain a form higher than the living soul. This, however, is possible in man, in whom it strives for a higher form. The Divine Influence grudges nothing. It bestows on him a higher form, called material or passive intellect. Men differ from each other, because most of them are physically of different constitutions, and the intellect follows the latter. If his gall be yellowish, he is quick and alert; if blackish, he is quiet and sedate. The temperament follows the mixture of humours. If an individual is found of evenly balanced humour, which controls his contrasting dispositions, like the two scales of a balance in the hand of the person who weighs and regulates them by adding or subtracting at his will, such a person possesses without doubt a heart which is free from strong passions. He covets a degree of divine character above his own. He is perplexed, not knowing which inclination should have preponderance. He does not give way either to anger, or to lust, or to any other passion, but controls himself, and seeks divine inspiration to walk the right path. This is the person on whom the divine and prophetic spirit is poured out, if he is fit for prophecy, but if he stands below that degree, he is only endowed with inspiration. In the latter case he is a pious man, but no prophet. There is no niggardliness with God, who allows every one his due. Philosophers call the giver of this degree Active Intellect, and regard it as an angel below God. If a man's intellect is in conjunction with the former, this is called his paradise and lasting life.

11. Al Khazari: Give me a brief discourse on all this.

12. The Rebbi: The existence of the human soul is shown in living beings by motion and perception, in contradistinction to the movements of the elements. The cause of the former is called soul, or animal power. This is divided into three divisions. The first is that which is common to animal and plant-life, and is called vegetative power; the second, which is common to man and the rest of living beings, is called vital power; the third specific of man is called rational power. The nature of the soul in the comprehensive and generic sense is defined by the examination of its actions as issuing from the forms adhering to matter, but not from matter, inasmuch as it is matter only without form. The knife, for instance, does not cut inasmuch as it is a substance, but inasmuch as it has the form of a knife. In the same way the animal does not feel and move inasmuch as it is a substance, but inasmuch as it has the form of a living being. This is what is called soul. These forms are called perfections entelechies, because through them the structures of things become perfect. The soul is therefore a perfection. We distinguish a primary and a secondary perfection. The former is the principle of actions, the latter the nature of the actions which arise out of the principle. The soul is a primary perfection, because it is a principle from which something else, a secondary entelechy may issue forth. The entelechy is either entelechy to a corporate object, or entelechy to amorphous matter. The soul is entelechy to a corporate object. Corporate objects are either natural or artificial. The soul is first entelechy to a natural corporate object. A natural corporate object is either organic or inorganic, which means that it performs its actions either by means of organs or without them. The soul is entelechy to a natural corporate object, endowed with organs, and potentially with life, viz. a mainspring of potentially vivified actions, or susceptible to such. The next consequence is that the soul is not the result of a combination of elements of substance. If a thing arises from a combination of component parts, one or more of these component parts preponderate, its form shapes itself accordingly. Or the component parts struggle with one another, so that not one of them retains its form, but their medium yields a new form. The soul which is not composed of corporeal ingredients is therefore nothing but external form, like the impression made by the seal in the clay which is composed of water and earth. The seal is not the result of the forms of water and earth. The first of the vegetative powers is that of nutrition, which forms, so to speak, the beginning, whilst that of propagation forms the end. The faculty of growth is in the middle, linking the beginning to the end. The faculty of propagation occupies the first place, and although it appears to be placed at the end, it rules supreme over the substance which is fitted to receive life. Assisted by growth and nutrition, it clothes it with the intended form. It then leaves the further management to the latter two till the moment of propagation. Propagation is aided, nutrition aids, growth aids and is aided. Nutrition has those four well-known powers at its disposal. Everything that moves does so by the will of a perception; otherwise, perception were useless. Providence, however, produces nothing that is either useless or injurious. Neither does it withhold anything that is necessary or useful.

Kuzari — Fifth Essay

Even mollusks, though apparently lying quietly, can contract and stretch themselves, and if placed on their backs, move till they turn over on their bellies, in order to reach their food. The exterior senses are thus known. As to the interior ones, the first is the general sense, because that which is useful or injurious can only be learnt by experience. God therefore gave man the faculty of conception, that he may grasp by it means the forms of objects perceived. This is what is meant under the term general sense. Then He gave him the faculty of remembering, to retain the notions of things perceived; further, the power of imagination, in order to restore what had been lost to memory; the faculty of judgment, in order to pause again and again at the new products of imagination, correct or false, till it is restored to memory. Lastly, He endowed him with the power of motion, in order to procure what is required from near and far, and to remove what is injurious. All the powers of a living being are either perceptive or motive. The motive power is of optative character, and is divided into two classes, viz. firstly moving to obtain what is desired, avidity; secondly, moving to repel what is undesirable, dislike. Perception is also divided into two classes, viz. external faculties, as the external senses; and internal faculties, as the internal senses. The motive power acts on the judgment of conception and with the assistance of imagination. It forms the extreme limit of animal life; for the motive power fails it in restoring the causes of perception and imagination. It is only endowed with the sense of instinct to regulate the causes of motion. Rational beings, on the other hand, are endowed with motion in order to obtain the rational soul, which has action and memory. The five senses, as is known, offer the means of perceiving form, number, size, motion, and rest. The existence of the common sense is explained if we, for instance, judge when we find honey that it is sweet. This is only possible because we possess a faculty common to the five senses, viz., the perceptive power, which is active both in waking and sleeping. To this is added a faculty which either combines all that which is united in the common sense, or separates, and fixes their differences without, however, depriving forms of the common sense. This is the faculty of imagination which is sometimes correct, sometimes incorrect, whilst the faculty of perception is always correct. The next is the faculty of judgment, which is of a deciding character, and judges whether an object is desirable or undesirable. The faculties of perception and imagination can neither judge nor decide, but can only picture an object. The faculty of recollection retains the objects it has perceived, that the wolf is an enemy, and the child beloved. Love and hatred, belief and unbelief belong to the realm of judgment. Memory retains that which

Kuzari Fifth Essay

the faculty of judgment declares to be true. The faculty of imagination is so called when in the service of judgment, but if employed by reason, it is called cogitation. The seat of the faculty of perception is in the fore part of the brain, that of imagination in the middle, that of memory at the back. The seat of judgment is in the whole brain, principally at the border line of the faculty of imagination. All these faculties perish with their organs, and no duration is granted to reasonable beings, although it claims the nucleus, so to speak, of these faculties as its own, and renders their real character manifest. This is the result of the philosopher's discourses on that which is beneath the rational soul. They call the soul hylic intellect, potential intellect, because it resembles matter which forms the connecting link between nothingness and actuality; in other words, all potential objects. They obtain rational forms either by way of divine inspiration or by application. Those obtained by inspiration are the result of original conception shared by all human beings guided by nature. Those acquired by application are gained by speculation and dialectic corollary. The result is the formation of logical conclusions, as species, classes, divisions, specialities, words simple and composed in various ways; compound conclusions true or untrue; propositions from which arise either apodictic, dialectic, rhetoric, sophistic, or poetic conclusions. There arise further the establishment of physical notions, as matter, form, nothingness, nature, place, time, motion, spherical and elementary substances, growth and decay in general; the origin of meteorological, mineral and terrestrial phenomena, as plants and animals; the essence of man; the nature of the soul according to its own conception; further, things mathematical, such as arithmetic, geometry, music, astronomy; further, things metaphysical, such as the knowledge of beginning and existence as such in general, and the accessories thereof either potential or actual, principle, cause, substance, accident, species and class, contrast and connaturality, congruence and difference, unity and plurality; the establishment of the principles of speculative subjects, as mathematics, natural history, from logic, all of which can only be gained by a knowledge of the last-named; further, the establishment of the existence of the Prime Creator, of the universal soul, the nature of species, the relation of the intellect to the Creator, the relation of the soul to the intellect, the relation of nature to the soul, the relation of matter and form to nature, the relation of the spheres, stars and other phenomena to matter and form. Then we must consider why they are constructed with such differences of sequence, the knowledge of divine guidance, of universal nature, of divine providence. The rational soul sometimes derives certain forms from the senses by applying to its own needs perception and memory, and making use of imagination and judgment. We shall then find that these forms have some attributes in common, but that they differ in others; some of these attributes are essential, others accidental. The soul divides or combines, and produces species, categories, divisions, specialities, and accidences. It then combines them by means of syllogisms, and produces satisfactory conclusions with the assistance of the universal intellect. Although, at first, it reposed on the faculties of perception, it does not require them for the formation of the ideas themselves, nor in the composition of the syllogisms, be it to verify them, or to form a conception. Just as the faculties of perception only acquire something relative to the object perceived, thus the intellectual faculties only conceive something relative to the conceived object, by abstracting the form from the matter, and remaining attached to the former. The faculty of perception, however, does not act spontaneously as does the rational soul, but it requires the motive power as well as the assistance of intermediaries which establish a connexion between the forms and itself. The power of intellect conceives spontaneously and conceives itself as often as it desires. The faculty of perception is therefore called passive, but the power of intellect is called active. Actual reason is nothing but the abstract of objects conceived, potentially existing in reason itself and rendered actual by the same. It is therefore also said that actual reason comprehends and is comprehended simultaneously. It is one of the special characteristics of reason that, by means of synthesis and analysis it transforms plurality into unity and unity into plurality. Although the activity of reason in combining proportions by means of careful consideration appears to require a certain time, the deduction of the conclusion is not dependent on time, reason itself being above time. When the rational soul turns its attention towards science, its activity is called theoretical reason. If, however, it undertakes to subdue animal instincts, its activity is called guidance, and it assumes the name of practical reason. Some people's reasoning power succeeds in establishing so intimate a connexion with the universal reason, that it is lifted above logical conclusions and meditation, escaping such necessity by inspiration and revelation. This special distinction is styled sanctity, or holy spirit. A proof that the soul is real, though incorporeal and no accessory, is to be found in the circumstance that it is the form of a corporeal object. According to its nature it cannot be divided like a corporeal object, or like an accessory when the substratum of the same is divided. Colour, smell, taste, heat and cold are divided as soon as their substrata are divided, though their nature is indivisible. The form of the intellect consists in the object conceived. A human being's conception cannot be divided, because half, or a piece of a human being cannot be styled man, although part of a corporeal object, or a colour can retain their names. Colour and corporeal object, if only existing in conception, allow no division even in thought. One cannot say: Half of a conceived colour, or half of a conceived corporeal object, as one can say: Half of this object is perceived, or Half of the colour borne by it and referring to it. One cannot speak of half of Zeid's soul, as one can speak of half of his body; for the former can neither be limited locally, nor defined in any way, nor pointed to. Now if it cannot be either a corporeal object nor an accessory borne by a corporeal object, its existence is manifested by its activity. There remains nothing but to see in it a substance with an existence of its own, endowed with angelic attributes and divine substantiality. Its primary tools are those spiritual forms which shape themselves in the centre of the brain from the psychical spirit by means of the power of imagination. The latter gives the faculty of reflecting, as soon as it becomes predominant enough to produce synthetical and analytical knowledge. It had been imaginative prior to this, when judgment was predominant in it, as is the case with children, animals, and with people whose constitution has been tried by illness. As a consequence, the human soul is deprived of those formations on account of the synthetical and analytical processes which are required for the unimpaired consideration of an opinion. In such a case the opinion becomes a defective judgment, wholly or partially. A proof that the soul is distinct from the body, and does not require it, is to be found in the circumstance that the physical powers are weakened by strong influences. The organ of the eye is damaged by the sun, and the ear by too strong a sound. The rational soul, however, retains whatever stronger knowledge it has obtained. Moreover, old age attacks the body, but not the soul. The latter is stronger after the fiftieth year, whilst the body is on the decline. The activity of the body is limited, which is not the case with that of the soul, for geometrical, arithmetical, and logical forms are unlimited. There now remains to be shown that there exists a spiritual substance, distinct from the body, which stands in the same relation to the soul as the light to the eye, and as soon as the soul is separated from the body, it is united to that substance. The soul does not gain its knowledge empirically. For the results of experience cannot be judged apodictically. No one can assert apodictically that no man can move his ears, just as we may judge that every human being feels; that every one who feels, lives; that every one who lives is a substance; that the whole is larger than a part, and other fundamental truths. For our belief in the correctness of opinions is not regulated by instruction, otherwise we should come to an endless chain of conclusions. But then the rational soul comes into connexion with the divine emanation. As long as this divine emanation is not defined by the general spiritual form, it cannot impregnate the soul with it. Every being possessed of an essentially spiritual form is an incorporeal substance. If this be so, this emanation is a spiritual, incorporeal substance, with an existence of its own. The conception which the soul has of the form is a perception entelechy for it. It would succeed in coming into contact with the spiritual substance, if its intimacy with the body did not interfere. A complete connexion is, however, impossible, unless all physical powers are subdued. For it is the body alone which prevents this connexion. As soon as the soul is separated from it, it becomes perfect, connected with what renders it immune to injury, and united with the noble substance which is styled the higher knowledge. All other powers only act for the body, and perish together with organs. The rational soul, however, having fashioned them, appropriated their kernel, as has been explained before.

13. Al Khazari: This philosophical discourse appears to be more accurate and truer than others.

14. The Rebbi: I feared that thou wouldst be deceived, and acquiesce in their views. Because they furnish mathematical and logical proofs, people accept everything they say concerning physics and metaphysics, taking every word as evidence. Didst thou not, from the very beginning, doubt their theories of the four elements, their search of the fire world, in which they place the aetherial fire, which is colourless, and therefore prevent the colour of the sky and stars from being seen. When did we ever accept an elementary fire? The highest degree of heat, if found in the earth, appears as coal; in the air as flame; in the water at boiling point. When did we ever witness an igneous or atmospheric substance entering into the substance of the plant or animal, and asserted that it was composed of all four elements, viz. fire, air, water, and earth? Supposing we did perceive water and earth enter the substance of a plant in altered form; but air and heat only assisted the process through their quality, but not as igneous and atmospheric bodies. Or when did we ever see them dissolved into the four real elements? If a part is reduced to a kind of dust, it is not real dust, but ashes, which can be used for healing purposes. Another part which is reduced to a kind of water is not real water, but an expressed liquid, a juice either poisonous or nourishing, but not drinkable water. The portion which is dissolved into a kind of air is vapour or fume, but no air fit to be breathed. Sometimes they alter their condition when absorbed by an animal or a plant, or enter a combination with earthly particles, move from alteration to alteration, but only in rare cases are they reduced to the pure element. Science, it is true, forces us to accept the theory that heat, cold, moisture, and dryness are primary qualities, the influences of which nobody can escape; that reason reduces compound things to them, or declares them to be composed of them; and places substances at their disposal which bear them, calling them fire, air, water, and earth. This is, however, but a conception and nomenclature, but it does not mean that they can emerge from mere theory into reality, and produce, by combination, all existing things. How can philosophers make such an assertion, whilst teaching the eternity of matter, and that man never arose otherwise than from issue and blood, blood from food, food from vegetables, and vegetables, as we have said, from seeds and water transformed with the assistance of sunlight, air, and earth. All stars and spherical constellations also exercise their influence. This is the objection to the view of philosophers concerning the elements. According to the Torah, it was God who created the world, together with animals and plants. There is no need to presuppose intermediaries or combinations of elements. If we make creation a postulate, all that is difficult becomes easy, and all that is crooked straight, as soon as one assumes that this world once did not exist, but came into existence by the will of God at the time He desired. Why dost thou trouble to examine the way in which bodies arose and were equipped with souls? Why art thou reluctant to accept the 'firmament' and 'the water above the heavens,' and the evil spirits mentioned by the Sages, the description of the events to be expected during the days of the MASHIACH, the resurrection of the dead and the world to come? Why should we need such artificial theories in order to prove the life of the soul after the dissolution of the body, considering that we have reliable information with regard to the return of the soul, be it spiritual or corporeal. If thou wouldst endeavour to confirm or refute these views logically, life would be spent in vain. Who vouchsafes the truth of the theory quoted above, that the soul is a spiritual substance which cannot be encompassed by space, and which is not subject to growth and decay? In what way differs my soul from thine, or from the Active Intellect, from other causes and the Prime Cause? Why, also, did not Aristotle's soul become united to that of Plato, either of them knowing the other's belief and innermost thought? Why do not all philosophers conceive their notions simultaneously, as is the case with God and the Active Intellect? How can they be subject to forgetfulness, and require reflection for every single one of their notions? Why is not a philosopher conscious of himself when he is asleep or intoxicated, or is prostrate with pleurisy, or has brain fever, or is old and decrepit? How should we judge a person who, having arrived at the extreme limit of philosophic speculation, is stricken by melancholy or depression, which makes him forget all his knowledge? Is he not himself in his eyes, or shall we say that he is some one else? Suppose he recovers gradually from his complaint, and begins to learn over again, but becomes old without having reached the former extent of his knowledge, has he two souls, the one different from the other? Suppose, further, that his temperament undergoes a change in the direction of love, ambition, or desire, shall I say that he has one soul in paradise and another in hell? Which are the limits of metaphysical knowledge by means of which the human soul is separated from the body without perishing? If this is the complete knowledge of existing things, much remains of which philosophers are ignorant concerning heaven, earth, and ocean. If one, however, must be satisfied with partial knowledge, then every rational soul exists separate, because primary notions are implanted in it. But if the isolated existence of the soul is based on the conception of the Ten Categories, or higher still, on the principles of intuition, in which all existing things are included ready to be grasped logically without following up all details, so is this a knowledge easily acquirable in one day. It would be strange if man could become an angel in one day. If it is incumbent to go the whole length and comprehend all these things in logical and scientific study, then the matter is unattainable and ends, in their opinion, infallibly in the death of the one who pursues it. Now thou didst allow thyself to be deceived by injurious fancies, didst seek that which thy Creator did not grant thee, and to obtain which no facilities have been granted to human nature. Only a few privileged individuals are allowed to grasp such things on the conditions mentioned before. These are the souls which comprehend the whole universe, know their Lord and His angels; who see one another, and know each other's secrets, as the prophet says: I, too, know it; be ye silent. We others, however, would not know how and by what means this came to pass, unless by way of prophecy. If what philosophers know of the matter were true, they would surely acquire it, since they discourse on the souls and prophecy. They are, however, like ordinary mortals. As regards human wisdom, they indeed occupy a high rank, as Socrates said: O my people, I do not deny your knowledge of the gods, but I confess that I do not understand it. As for me, I am only wise in human matters. Philosophers justify their recourse to speculation by the absence of prophecy and divine light. They established the demonstrative sciences on a broad and unlimited basis, and on that account separated without either agreeing or disagreeing with each other concerning that on which they held such widely diverging views later on in metaphysics, and occasionally in physics. If there exists a class representing one and the same view, this is not the result of research and investigation, but because they belong to the same philosophic school in which this was taught, as the schools of Pythagoras, Empedocles, Aristotle, Plato, or others, as the Academy and Peripatetics, who belong to the school of Aristotle. They start with views which deprecate reason, but are deprecated by the latter. An example of this is their explanation of the cause of the revolution of the sphere, and the endeavour of the latter to remedy its imperfection, so as to be absolutely exact on all sides. As, however, this is not always possible and, in all points, it tries to revolve the opposite way. They contrived similar theories with regard to the emanations from the Prime Cause, viz., that from the intuition of the first cause an angel arose; and from its knowledge of itself a sphere arose, and thence downward in eleven degrees, until the emanation arrived at the Active Intellect, from which neither an angel nor a sphere developed. All these things are still less satisfactory than the "Book of Creation." They are full of doubts, and there is no consensus of opinion between one philosopher and another. Yet they cannot be blamed, nay, deserve thanks for all they have produced in abstract speculations. For their intentions were good; they observed the laws of reason, and led virtuous lives. At all events, they have earned this praise, because the same duties were not imposed on them as they were on us when we were given revelation, and a tradition which is tantamount to revelation.

15. Al Khazari: Give me a brief abstract of the views rife among the doctors of theology, whom the Karaites style: The Masters of the Kalam.

16. The Rebbi: This would be of no use; it would merely be an exercise in the dialectics of the Kalam, and a lesson on the Rebbinic sentence: Be careful to learn what answer to give to an Epicurean. The consummate philosopher, like the prophet, can only impart little to another person in the way of instruction, and cannot refute his objections dialectically. As to the master of Kalam, learning sheds its lustre on him, thereby inducing his hearers to place him above the pious and immaculate whose learning consists in principles of a creed which allow of no refutation. The final aim of the Mutakallim in everything he learns and teaches is that these principles of creed enter his soul as well as that of his disciples in the same natural form as they exist in the soul of the pious person. In some cases, the art of the Kalam does him greater harm than the principles of truth, because it teaches doubts and traditional prejudices. We experience a similar thing with people who apply themselves to prosody and practice scanning metres. There we can hear braying and a babel of words in an art which offers no difficulties to those naturally gifted. The latter enjoy making verses in which no fault can be found. The aim of the former class is to be like the latter who appear ignorant of the art of verse-making, because they cannot learn what the others are able to teach. The naturally gifted person, however, can teach one similarly endowed with the slightest hint. In the same manner sparks are kindled in the souls of people naturally open to religion and approachment to God, by the words of the pious, sparks which become luminaries in their hearts, whilst those who are not so gifted must have recourse to the Kalam. He often derives no benefit from it, nay, he comes to grief over it.

17. Al Khazari: I do not expect an exhaustive discourse on this subject, but I ask thee for some abstracts like those given to me before. For thou didst strike my ear, and my soul yearns for it.

18. The Rebbi: The **FIRST** Axiom: deals with

the creation of the world, with the object of making it an established fact, and it denies the theory that it is without beginning. If time had no beginning, the number of individuals existing in the past down to our own age would be endless. That which is endless cannot be actual. How could those individuals have become actual, being so many as to be without number? There is no doubt, however, that the past had a beginning, and that the existing individuals are limited by a number. It is within the power of the human mind to count thousands or millions multiplied without end, at least in theory, but this cannot be done in reality. For that which becomes actual and can be counted as one, is like the number which is both actual and finite without doubt. How can the infinite become actual? The world has, therefore, a beginning, and the revolutions of the spheres are subject to a finite number. Further, that which is infinite can neither be halved nor doubled, nor subjected to any arithmetical calculation. We are aware that the revolutions of the sun are one-twelfth of those of the moon, and that the other movements of spheres stand in similar relation to each other, one being the divisor of the other. The infinite, however, has no divisor. How could the one be like the other, which is infinite, being either below or above it, I mean larger or smaller in number? How could the infinite come to us? If an infinite number of things existed before us, how could the [idea of] number come to us? If a thing has an end, it must also have had a beginning, otherwise each individual object must have waited for the [prior] existence of an infinite number of others; so, none would ever come into existence. **SECOND** Axiom: The world is created, because it is a corporeal object. A corporeal object cannot be conceived without movement and rest, which are both attributes of accessory but not simultaneous character. That which is accessory must be newly made in accordance with its very nature. That which preceded has also been created. For had it been eternal, it could not have been non-existent. Consequently both [motion and rest] are created. A thing that cannot exist without newly created accessories is created itself, because it could not have been preceded by its accessories. If the latter are created, the former must be so likewise. **THIRD** Axiom: Every created object must have a cause which created it. For the created object is connected with a certain time, irrespective of an earlier or later epoch. The circumstance that it is encompassed by a specific time, irrespective of the period, renders a specificator necessary. **FOURTH** Axiom: God is eternal, without beginning and without end. For had He been created, He would require a Creator. This would result in a chain of conclusions without end, until we came to the first Creator, whom we look for. **FIFTH** AXIOM: God is everlasting, and will never cease to exist. For a being proved to be without beginning cannot have had a nonexistence. Nonexistence must have a cause, just as the disappearance of a thing from existence must also have a cause. Nothing vanishes from existence on its own account, but on account of its contrast. God, however, has neither a contrast nor his equal. For if anything were like Him in every respect, it would be Himself, but He cannot be described as twofold. The thing which causes nonexistence cannot be without beginning, as has been explained before in connexion with the eternity of God's existence. He cannot, therefore, be a created Being, because everything newly arising must have its cause in the eternal Being. But how can the thing caused make its cause disappear. **SIXTH** AXIOM: God is not corporeal. A corporeal object cannot be free from new accessories. A thing that is not free from new accessories is created. God cannot be called accidence, because the accidence cannot exist except on a substratum. The accidence is caused by the corporeal object by which it is attracted and borne. God, however, cannot be defined by a particular outline or place, since this is the characteristic of a corporeal object. **SEVENTH** Axiom: God knows all that is great or small, and nothing escapes His omniscience. For it has been shown that He created, arranged, and instituted everything, as it is written: He that planted the ear, shall He not hear; He that formed the eye, shall He not see. Further, Yea, darkness hideth not from Thee, etc., and For Thou hast created my reins. **EIGHTH** Axiom: God lives. His omniscience and omnipotence having been demonstrated; He must be living. His life, however, is not like ours, created with senses and movement, but a life of pure reason. His life and He are identical. **NINTH** Axiom: God has will. For it is in His power to issue forth the opposite of all He caused to exist, or its non-existence, or anticipation, or postponement. His omnipotence is the same in any case. There must exist a will which fixes His omnipotence on one of these issues to the exclusion of the other. One might also say that His omniscience can spare both His omnipotence and will. In this case His omniscience would be identical with one particular time and issue, and His eternal omniscience would be the cause of every existing being just as it is. This agrees with the view of philosophers. **TENTH** Axiom: The divine will is without beginning, and corresponds to His omniscience. Nothing in it can be renewed or altered. He is living through the very life of His nature, but not by means of an acquired life. He is omnipotent through His own power, has will through His own will. For the coexistence of a thing and that which negatives it is impossible. One cannot therefore say in a general way: Omnipotent without power.

19. Al Khazari: This is sufficient to refresh my memory. There is no doubt that thy discourse on the soul and reason, as well as these axioms, was quoted from other authorities. Now I desire to hear thy own opinion and principles of faith. Thou didst declare thy willingness to examine this and similar points. It seems to me that it will not be possible to omit the questions of predestination and human free will, since they are of actual importance. Now tell me thy mind.

20. The Rebbi: Only a perverse, heretical person would deny the nature of what is possible, making assertions of opinions in which he does not believe. Yet from the preparations he makes for events he hopes for or fears, one can see that he believes in their possibility, and that his preparations may be useful. If he believed in absolute necessity, he would simply submit, and not equip himself with weapons against his enemy, or with food against his hunger. If he, on the other hand, thinks that either preparation or the omission of the same is necessary in accordance with the nature of the case, he admits intermediary causes, as well as their consequences. He will encounter his desire in every intermediary cause, and if he is just and not perverse, he will find himself placed between himself and his desire to obtain achievable objects, which he can pursue or abandon as he likes. Such a belief is not incompatible with a belief in Divine Providence, but everything is led back to him in various ways, as I am going to explain. My opinion is that everything of which we are conscious is referred to the Prime Cause in two ways, either as an immediate expression of the divine will, or through intermediaries. An instance of the first kind is found in the synthetic arrangement visible in animals, plants and spheres, objects which no intelligent observer would trace back to accident, but to a creative and wise will, which gives everything its place and portion. An instance of the second kind is to be found in the burning of a beam. Fire is a fine, hot, and active substance, whilst wood is a porous and passive one. It is the nature of the fine and active substance to affect its object, whilst heat and dryness warm and volatilize the moisture of the object till it is completely dissolved. If thou seekest the causes of these processes, active as well as passive, thou wilt not fail to discover them. Thou mayest even discover the causes of their causes till thou arrivest at the spheres, then at their causes, and finally at the Prime Cause. One might justly say that everything is ordained by God, and another is equally right in making men free will or accident responsible for it, without, however, bringing it outside the divine providence. If thou likest thou mayest render the matter more intelligible by means of the following classification. Effects are either of divine or of natural origin, either accidental or arbitrary. The divine ones issue forth actively, having no other causes except God's will. The natural ones are derived from intermediate, preparatory causes which bring them to the desired end, as long as no obstacle arises from one of the other three classes. The accidental ones are likewise the result of intermediary causes, but accidentally, not by nature or arrangement, or by will power. They are not prepared to be brought to completion and standstill, and they stand apart from the other three classes. As regards the arbitrary actions, they have their roots in the free will of man, when he is in a position to exercise it. Free will belongs to the class of intermediary causes, and possesses causes which reduce it, chainlike, to the Prime Cause. This course is not compulsory, because the whole thing is potential, and the mind wavers between an opinion and its opposite, being permitted to turn where it chooses. The result is praise or blame for the choice, which is not the case in the other classes. An accidental or natural cause cannot be blamed, although some of them admit a possibility. But one cannot blame a child or a sleeping person for harm done. The opposite was possible just the same, and they cannot be blamed, because they lack judgment. Dost, thou think that those who deny the potential are not wroth with those who injure them purposely. Or do they acquiesce in being robbed of their garments, and consequently also in suffering from cold, just as they would expose themselves to the north wind on a cold day? Or do they believe that the anger about it is but a fallacious exertion, instituted for no purpose, that man may feel anger about one particular thing, or give praise and blame, show hatred etc.? In these cases, free will, as such, has no forcing cause, because it is itself reduced to compulsion. Man's language, then, would be as little free as the beating of his pulse. This would be against evident appearances. Thou perceivest that speaking or being silent is in thy power as long as thou art in possession of thy reason, and not controlled by other casualties. If all incidents would be the result of the original will of the Prime Cause, they would, each in its turn, be created anew in every moment. We might then say that the Creator created anew the whole world this very moment. The servant of God would be no better than the wicked, as both would be obedient, and only do that for which they are fated. A conviction of this kind has many objections, whilst the refutation of appearances is most difficult, as we said before. The objection made against those who assert that some matters are removed from the bounds of Providence by human free will is to be refuted by what was said before, viz. that they are completely outside the control of Providence, but are indirectly linked to it. There is still another objection, viz. that these matters are outside the divine omniscience, because the absolutely potential is naturally an unknown quantity. The Mutakallims considered this matter in detail, with the result that the divine knowledge of the potential is but casual, and that the knowledge of a thing is neither the cause of its coming into existence, nor of its disappearance therefrom. There is, withal, a possibility of existence and non-existence. For the knowledge of events to come is not the cause of their existence, just as is the case with the knowledge of things which have been. This is but a proof that the knowledge belongs to God, or to the angels, or the prophets, or the priests. If this knowledge were the cause of the existence of a thing, many people would be placed in paradise solely for the sake of the divine knowledge that they are pious, even if they have done no pious act. Others would be in Gehenna, because God knows them to be wicked, without their having committed a sin. Man should also be satisfied without having eaten, because he knows that he is accustomed to be satisfied at certain times. Another consequence would be that intermediary causes would cease to exist, and their disappearance would be shared by that of the intermediary factors. This renders the following verse intelligible: And God did prove Abraham, in order to render his theoretical obedience practical, and let it be the cause of his prosperity. He says subsequently "Because thou hast done this thing... I will bless thee". Now since events must be either of divine origin, or arise out of one of the other classes, and the possibility exists that they are all providential, the people preferred to refer them all to God, because this encourages belief most effectually. He, however, who knows how to distinguish one people from another, one person from another, one time from another, one place from another, and certain circumstances from others, will perceive that heavenly dictated event mostly came to pass in the chosen and holy land, and among the privileged Israelitish people, and in that time and under circumstances which were accompanied by laws and customs the observation of which was beneficial, whilst their neglect wrought harm. Matters natural or accidental were of no avail against the undesired effect, nor could they do harm at the time of pious conduct. For this reason, Israelites serve every religion as evidence against the heretics who followed the view of the Grecian Epicurus, viz. that all things are the outcome of accidents, since no settled purpose is ever discernible in them. His school is called that of the Hedonists, because they held the opinion that pleasure is the desired aim and goodness absolute. The endeavour of him who observes a lawgiver's regulations is to find favour in his eyes, and to place his desires before him. He seeks inspirations if he is pious, or miracles if he is a prophet, or if his people enjoy the divine pleasure on the basis of the conditions of time, place and action, as put down in the Torah. He need not be concerned about natural or accidental causes, since he knows that he is protected from their evil consequences, either through preceding instruction which drives the evil away, or through some wonderful incident which is collateral with that evil. The good issuing from accidental causes is not denied to the sinner, much less to the virtuous. Happy events occurring to the wicked have their origin only in those accidental and natural causes, but no one can ward off threatening calamities. The good, on the contrary, prosper through the same causes, whilst being protected from misfortune. But I have diverged a little from my subject. Returning to the same, I say that David laid down three causes of death, viz. God may slay him, divine cause; Or his day shall come to die, natural cause; Or he shall descend into battle and perish, accidental cause. He omits the fourth possibility, viz. suicide, because no rational being seeks death voluntarily. If Saul killed himself, it was not to seek death, but to escape torture and derision. A similar classification can be made with regard to speech. The speech of a prophet at the time when he is enwrapped by the Holy Spirit is in every part directed by the Divine

Influence, the prophet himself being powerless to alter one word. Natural speech consists in communications and hints which conform to the subject to be discussed, and the mind follows without previous convention. Conventional languages are composed of natural and arbitrary elements. Accidental speech is that of a madman, and is neither in harmony with a subject, nor to the purpose. Free speech is that of a prophet when not inspired, or the words of an intelligent, thinking person who connects his words, and chooses his expressions in accordance with the subject under consideration. If he wished he could replace each word by another, could even drop the whole subject and take up another. All these cases, however, can be reduced indirectly to God, but not as immediate issues of the Prime Will, otherwise the words of a child, and mad people, the speech of an orator, and the song of a poet were the words of God. Far be this from Him. The excuse of a slothful person who tells the energetic one that that which is to be, exists previously in the knowledge of God, is inconclusive. For should he even assert that that which shall be must be, he is told: Quite so; but this argument should not prevent thee to take the best counsel, to prepare weapons against thy enemy, and food for hunger, as soon as thou art aware that that both thy safety and destruction depend upon intermediary causes. One of them, which is the most

Kuzari — Fifth Essay

frequent, is the application of energy and industry, or of lassitude and indolence. Do not try to refute me with those rare and accidental cases, viz. that a circumspect person perishes, whilst the careless and unprotected one is saved. For the word safety means something quite different from the word risk. A sensible person will not flee from a place of safety to one of risk, just as one flees from a dangerous place to a safe one. If safety accrues in the place of danger this is considered rare, but if a person perishes in a safe place, it is called an extraordinary occurrence. One should, therefore, employ circumspection. One of the causes of carelessness is the view opposite to this advice. Everything, however, is indirectly related to God. Whatever happens through direct ordination belongs to the class of strange and miraculous events, and can dispense with intermediary causes. In some cases, they are, however, necessary, as in the preservation of Moshe during his fast of forty days, when he was without food, or in the destruction of Sanherib's army without a visible cause-unless through a divine one-which we cannot consider as such, as we do not know what it is. Of such we say that preparation avails them not, viz. preparation in the concrete sense. Moral preparation, however, based on the secret of the law, benefits him who knows and understands it, because it brings what is good, and repels what is bad. If man aids intermediary causes with energy, having left to God the objects of his fear with a pure mind, he fares well, and suffers no loss. He, however, who courts danger transgresses the warning: You shall not tempt the Lord, in spite of his confidence in God. But if one considers it absurd, to give commands to a person who, as he knows beforehand, may either disobey or obey him, this is not absurd. We have shown previously that disobedience and obedience depend upon intermediary causes. The cause of obedience is the command for it. The obeying person knew beforehand that he would do so and that the cause of it was that he had heard reproof. He also keeps in mind that disobedience depends on intermediary causes, which are to be found either in the companionship of wicked people, or in the preponderance of evil temperament, or inclination for comfort and rest. Finally, he knew that his disobedience was lessened through reproof. Reproof, as is known, impresses the mind in any case, and even the soul of an insubordinate person is in some small way influenced by reproof. In a higher degree this takes place in a multitude, because there is at any rate one person to be found who accepts it. Far from being useless, reproof is, therefore, useful.

The **FIRST PRINCIPLE**, containing the confirmation of the above-mentioned advice, establishes the existence of the Prime Cause. God is the wise Creator; in whose works nothing is useless. They are all founded upon His wisdom and an order which suffers no deterioration. Whoever contemplates this must find the conviction of the greatness of His creation deeply rooted in his mind. This results in the belief that no flaw can be found in His works. If in some minor matter a fault seems apparent, his belief is not shaken, but he ascribes it to his own ignorance and defective intelligence.

The **SECOND PRINCIPLE**, admits the existence of intermediary causes, which, however, are not active, but causes, either in the way of substance matter or instruments. Issue and blood are the materials of which man is formed, connected by the organs of propagation. The spirit and faculties are tools which employ them under the will of God, in order to produce a formation perfect in proportion, form and nurture. Intermediary causes are necessary for every created thing, as the dust which was required for the creation of Adam. It is therefore not superfluous to assume the existence of intermediary causes.

The **THIRD PRINCIPLE**, God gives every substance the best and most appropriate form. He is the All-benevolent, who does not withhold His goodness, wisdom, and guidance from anything. His wisdom visible in the flea and gnat is not less than in the order of the spheres The difference of things is the outcome of their substances. One cannot, therefore, ask:

Kuzari — Fifth Essay

Why did He not create me an angel, just as little as the worm can ask: Why didst Thou not create me a human being.

The **FOURTH PRINCIPLE**, expresses the conviction that existing beings are of higher or lower degree. Everything that is possessed of feeling and perception is higher than those creatures which lack the same, since the former are nearer the degree of the Prime Cause which is Reason itself. The lowest plant occupies a higher rank than the noblest mineral, the lowest animal is higher than the noblest plant, and the lowest human being is higher than the noblest animal. Thus, the lowest follower of the divine law occupies a higher place than the noblest heathen. For the divine law confers something of the nature of angels on the human mind, a thing which cannot be acquired otherwise. The proof is that prolonged practice of this law leads up to the degree of prophetic inspiration, than which there is no nearer degree to God for man. A froward monotheist is, therefore, preferable to the pagan, because the divine law empowered him to lead an angelic life and to reach the degree of angels, though it has become sullied and defaced by his frowardness. Some traces will always remain, and the fire of his longing for it is not quite extinguished. If he had his own choice, he would prefer to remain untutored, just as a sick and pain-plagued person would not prefer to be a horse, or fish, or bird, which, though happy and free from pain, is far removed from reason which brings near to the divine degree.

The **FIFTH PRINCIPLE**, The mind of him who listens to the reproof of an adviser is impressed by it, if it is acceptable. True reproof is useful in any case, and although the evil doer may not be brought back from his bad ways, a spark is kindled in his soul by this reproof, and he sees that his deed is bad. This is part and beginning of repentance.

The **SIXTH PRINCIPLE**, Man finds in himself this power of doing evil or avoiding it in matters which are in his hand. Any failure in this respect is accounted for by the absence of intermediary causes, or his ignorance of them. If, for instance, a strange beggar, unacquainted with the art of governing, desires to become the ruler of a nation, one could not comply with his wish. Were he, however, possessed of the intermediary causes, and were he to know how to employ them, his desire would be justified, just as it would for an object the causes of which are at his disposal, and which he knows and controls when ruling his house, children, and servants or, in a higher degree, his limbs, which latter he can move as he chooses, whilst speaking as he likes; or, in a still higher degree, controlling his thoughts and imagining objects far and near in any way he likes. He is master over his intermediary causes. For a similar reason it is unlikely that the weak chess player should beat the strong one. One cannot speak of good or bad fortune in a game of chess, as in a war between two princes. For the causes of the game are open completely to study, and the expert will always be the conqueror. He need fear nothing in the ordinary way which can cause him great difficulty, neither need he fear anything accidental, except perhaps anything unusual arising from inattention. The last-named, however, comes under the name of ignorance, which was discussed before. This being so, everything can be traced back to the Prime Cause in the way intimated before. The Prime Will is visible in the history of the Israelites during the time when the Shekhinah dwelt among them. Afterwards it became doubtful, exeept in the hearts of the faithful, whether these even, were primarily caused by God or by spherical, or accidental causes. No decisive proof of this exists. It is, however, best to refer everything to God, particularly important events, such as death, victory, good and bad fortune, etc.

21. The Rebbi: This and similar subjects afford proper points for research, comprising as they do the character of the divine decrees concerning man, as intimated in the prophetic words: 'He visits the sin of the fathers on the children... of his enemies... and showing mercy unto thousands of them that love Him and keep His commandments. This means that every iniquity is remembered till the time of punishment comes, as laid down in the Torah and the teachings of the Sages; that some punishments can be warded off by repentance, and some not. It further includes the conditions of repentance, the trials, tribulations, and punishments for past transgressions winch visit man as retaliation in this world, or the next, or for paternal transgressions, and, finally, the good fortune which we enjoy as a reward for former pious actions, or the 'merit of the fathers, or which are sent to try us. These points of view are complicated by others and deeper ones, and there remains some doubt whether an examination will disclose the majority of causes of the misfortune of the just and the prosperity of the wicked. That which we cannot discover may be confidently left to God's omniscience and justice, and man must admit that he does not know the reasons, although they may lie on the surface, and still less can be known those which are really hidden. If man's contemplations lead him to the Prime Being and to the necessary attributes, he withdraws from it, because he sees a curtain of light which blinds the eye. We are debarred from perceiving it on account of our defective sight and narrow minds, but not because it is hidden or faulty. To those endowed with prophetic vision it appears too bright and resplendent to require any other proof. The culminating point of our appreciation of His nature is that we are able to distinguish supernatural causes in natural occurrences. This we ascribe to a non-corporeal and divine power, just as Galen, speaking of the forming power, places it above all other forces. In his opinion it did not arise out of certain combinations, but miraculously, by command of God, and we see substances changed, the course of nature altered, and new things produced without craft. This is the difference between the work of Moshe and that of the magicians whose secret art was open to discovery, just as Jeremiah says: They are vanity, the work of errors. He means to say that when they are closely examined, they appear vain as any contemptible thing. The Divine Influence, however, if investigated, appears as pure gold. If we have reached this degree, we say, that there is surely an incorporeal being which guides all corporeal substances, but which our mind is inadequate to examine. We therefore dwell on His works, but refrain from describing His nature. For if we were able to grasp it, this were a defect in Him. We take, however, no heed of the words of philosophers who divide the divine world into various degrees. As soon as we are free from our bodies there is for us only one divine degree. It is God alone who controls everything corporeal. The reason why philosophers adopted many gods is to be found in their investigations of the movements of the spheres, of which they counted more than forty. They found for every movement a separate cause, from which they concluded that these movements were independent rather than necessary or natural. Each movement, therefore, originated with a soul. Every soul has intellect, and this intellect is an angel severed from material substance. They called these intellects, or angels, or secondary causes and other names. The nethermost degree, nearest to us, is the Active Intelligence, of which they taught that it guided the nether world. The next is the Hylic Intellect, then comes the soul, nature, the natural and animal forces, and the faculties of each human organ. All these, however, are subtleties, and pleasant for investigation. He who is deceived by them is in any case a heretic. Leave also alone the argument of the Karaites, taken from David's last will to his son: And thou, Shlomo, my son, know thou the God of thy father, and serve Him. They conclude from this verse that a complete knowledge of God must precede His worship. As a matter of fact, David reminded his son to imitate his father and ancestors in their belief in the God of Abraham, Itzhak and Yaakov, whose solicitude was with them, and who fulfilled His promises in multiplying their descendants, gave them Palestine, and caused His Shekhinah to dwell among them. It is also written: 'Gods which ye did not know,' but this does not allude to the real truth, but those objects from which neither good nor evil can issue, and deserve neither confidence nor fear.

Kuzari — Fifth Essay

CONCLUSION OF THE BOOK

22 - The Rebbi was then concerned to leave the land of the Khazari and to betake himself to Jerusalem. The king was loth to let him go, and spoke to him in this sense as follows: What can be sought in Palestine nowadays, since the divine reflex is absent from it, whilst, with a pure mind and desire, one can approach God in any place. Why wilt thou run into danger. on land and water and among various peoples.

23. The Rebbi answered: The visible Shekhinah has, indeed, disappeared, because it does not reveal itself except to a prophet or a favoured community, and in a distinguished place. This is what we look for in the passage: Let our eyes behold when Thou returnest to Zion. As regards the invisible and spiritual Shekhinah, it is with every born Israelite of virtuous life, pure heart, and upright mind before the Lord of Israel. Palestine is especially distinguished by the Lord of Israel, and no function can be perfect except there. Many of the Israelitish laws do not concern those who do not live there; heart and soul are only perfectly pure and immaculate in the place which is believed to be specially selected by God. If this is true in a figurative sense, how much more-true in reality, as we have shown

Thus the longing for it is awakened with disinterested motives, especially for him who wishes to live there, and to atone for past transgressions, since there is no opportunity of bringing the sacrifices ordained by God for intentional and unintentional sins. He is supported by the saying of the Sages: Exile atones for sins, especially if his exile brings him into the place of God's choice. The danger he runs on land and sea does not come under the category of: You shall not tempt the Lord; but the verse refers to risks which one takes when travelling with merchandise in the hope of gain. He who incurs even greater danger on account of his ardent desire to obtain forgiveness is free from reproach if he has closed the balance of his life, expressed his gratitude for his past life, and is satisfied to spend the rest of his days in seeking the favour of his Lord. He braves danger, and if he escapes, he praises God gratefully. But should he perish through his sins, he has obtained the divine favour, and may be confident that he has atoned for most of his sins by his death. In my opinion this is better than to seek the dangers of war in order to gain fame and spoil by courage and bravery. This kind of danger is even inferior to that of those who march into war for hire.

24. Al Khazari: I thought that thou didst love freedom, but now I see thee finding new religious duties which thou wilt be obliged to fulfil in Palestine, which are, however, in abeyance here.

25. The Rebbi: I only seek freedom from the service of those numerous people whose favour I do not care for, and shall never obtain, though I worked for it all my life. Even if I could obtain it, it would not profit me-I mean serving men and courting their favour. I would rather seek the service of the One whose favour is obtained with the smallest effort, yet it profits in this world and the next. This is the favour of God, His service spells freedom, and humility before Him is true honour.

26. Al Khazari: If thou believest in all that thou sayest, God knows thy mind. The mind is free before God, who knows the hearts and discloses what is hidden.

27. The Rebbi: This is true when action is impossible. Man is free in his endeavours and work. But he deserves blame who does not look for visible reward for visible work. For this reason, it is written: Ye shall blow an alarm with the trumpets, and ye shall be remembered before the Lord your God. They shall be to you for a memorial. A memorial of blowing of trumpets. God need not be reminded, but actions must be perfect to claim reward. Likewise, must the ideas of the prayers be pronounced in the most perfect way to be considered as prayer and supplication. Now if thou bringest intention and action to perfection thou mayest expect reward. This is popularly expressed by reminding, and - the Torah speaks in the manner of human beings. If the action is minus the intention, or the intention minus the action, the expectation for reward is lost, except in impossible things. It is, however, rather useful to show the good intention if the deed is impossible, as we express this in our prayer: On account of our sins have we been driven out of our land. This sacred place serves to remind men and to stimulate them to love God, being a reward and promise, as it is written: Thou shalt arise and have mercy upon Zion, for the time to favour her, yea, the set time is come. For thy servants take pleasure in her stones and embrace the dust thereof. This means that Jerusalem can only be rebuilt when Israel yearns for it to such an extent that they embrace her stones and dust.

28. Al Khazari: If this be so, it would be a sin to hinder thee. It is, on the contrary, a merit to assist thee. May God grant thee His help, and be thy protector and friend. May He favour thee in His mercy.

www.ingramcontent.com/pod-product-compliance
Lightning Source LLC
Chambersburg PA
CBHW070127080526
44586CB00015B/1594